Vize

r. CONSOLATO GENERALE D'ITALIA

Costantinopoli

rilasciato al

Sig

titore del passaporto

BUONO PER IL SEMPLICE TRANSITO NEL
REGNO, PER UNA VOLTA SOLA. IL TITOLARE
NON PUO' SOFFERMARSI IN ITALIA OLTRE
IL TEMPO NECESSARIO AL TRANSITO STESSO.

Costantinopoli, li

Il R. Console Generale

REGNO D'ITALIA   REGNO D'ITALIA
MARCA CONSOLARE   MARCA CON

LIRE 0.05   LIRE   LIRE 0.

Hodgson, Barbara, 1955–
Italy out of hand : a
capricious tour /
c2005.
33305209970981
sa   09/15/05

Italy Out of Hand

A Capricious Tour

Barbara Hodgson

SANTA CLARA COUNTY LIBRARY

3 3305 20997 0981

Copyright © 2005 by Barbara Hodgson
No part of this book may be reproduced in any form
without written permission from the publisher.

All uncredited archival images are from Byzantium Archives.
Every effort has been made to trace accurate ownership of
copyrighted text and visual material used in this book.
Errors or omissions will be corrected in subsequent editions, provided notification is sent to the publisher. Page
192 constitutes a continuation of the copyright page.

LIBRARY OF CONGRESS CATALOGING-IN-PUBLICATION DATA available.
ISBN 0-8118-3146-9

Manufactured in China
Design by Barbara Hodgson/Byzantium Books

10 9 8 7 6 5 4 3 2 1

Chronicle Books LLC
85 Second Street
San Francisco, CA 94105

www.chroniclebooks.com

ENDPAPER: *Genoa's
Cimitero di Staglieno.*
p. i: *Visa to Italy, 1950.*
p. ii: *Map of Italy from
The Handy Atlas, c. 1905.*
pp. iv-v: *Statues from the
Palazzo dei Conservatori,
Rome, including Emperor
Constantine's hand.*
p. viii: *Postcard, c. 1915.*

ACKNOWLEDGMENTS
I'm deeply indebted to all the people who helped with Italian stories, facts,
and pictures. Special thanks to the following: Karen Elizabeth Gordon, for our
many conversations and for our forays into the Arezzo countryside; Peggy
Earle, for many consultations, book and image loans, and exchanges of ideas;
Laurent Budik, for the book loans and information on gelati; Rollin Milroy,
for information on Francesco Griffo and Amalfi; Nick Bantock, for the image
loans; Rosamond Purcell, for the loan of the Ravenna Monster; Finola Finlay
and Denis Murphy, for their invaluable help with the Latin; Stan Hodgson, for
his expertise on volcanic golf, even if we never ended up playing a round;
Joyce Williams and Don Clark of Joyce Williams Prints and Maps, for the
image loans; Don Stewart of MacLeod's Books, for loans of material; Todd
Belcher, for help with the photography; Victoria Steele, for pointing out the
beautiful church of Sant'Ivo alla Sapienza; Sarah Malarkey and Jodi Davis of
Chronicle Books, for their inextinguishable enthusiasm for this project; copy
editor Judith Dunham, for her rigorous attention and clarity; proofreader
Desne Ahlers, for her care, especially with the Italian; editor Annie Barrows,
for whipping this all into shape and for her bottomless well of knowledge for
all things musical, saintly, papal, and literary. A very special thanks to David
Gay, who continues to suffer, though never in silence.

Contents

THE WORDS *Napoli, binario due,* crackle and sputter out of the loudspeaker, barely comprehensible over the swell of voices on the crowded platform. The train to Naples is about to leave, and there doesn't seem to be a single seat available. So many passengers are standing that I can barely squeeze down the corridor. Wait, seats are free in this compartment. Why hasn't anyone else taken them? A young girl stands, her arm hanging out the window, her face crumpled into a portrait of misery. What on earth is she holding onto? A discreet glance reveals that she is clutching a clear plastic bag containing a large fish. As the train lurches out of the station, the bag begins to swing and, as we pick up speed, fish juice spatters the window. An unholy stink fills the compartment.

The mad crush and especially the vision of the airborne fish were my introduction to Italy. They set the tone for the many trips that followed but did little to prepare me for the improbable encounters that lay ahead: collisions—both cultural and literal—with saints' relics, amorous octogenarians, the grotesque folly of Palagonia, and Bernini's Baroque, to name but a few.

The Italy that I have come to know has given me a taste for the random and the bizarre and has compelled me to search out

Italia

"Now tell us what is Italy?"—Elizabeth Barrett Browning, 1851

When you travel in Italy, you'll find no lack of *ciceroni,* guides. Byron, for example, whom you'll meet often along the way, wrote this about his expertise: "I have *lived* among the Italians— not *Florenced,* and *Romed,* and galleried, and conversationed it for a few months . . . and you may be sure of what I say to you."

FACING PAGE: *Some of your guides. Top, left to right: Raphael, Vincenzo Bellini, Hester Piozzi (Mrs Thrale); center: Mary Shelley, Pietro Bembo, Gabriele D'Annunzio; bottom: Johann Wolfgang von Goethe, Charles Dickens, Ulisse Aldrovandi.*

the stories and images that contribute to its flamboyant character. My discoveries have led me to create *Italy Out of Hand,* a compendium of the ridiculous and the obscure. Unlike its predecessor *Paris Out of Hand,* in which Karen Elizabeth Gordon, Nick Bantock, and I played with our surrealistic and fictional imaginings of the famed city, *Italy Out of Hand* draws on long-accepted truths and legends, for in Italy, as you will see, truth is far stranger than fiction.

Exploring minutiae is a means of confronting a country that is too intricate and too inexplicable to tackle head on. Italy has seen so much and has been loved by so many that only the dusty corners reveal, and only for a moment, its essence.

This is not a guidebook; it has no hotels, and few restaurants, and all maps are at least 80 years old. *Italy Out of Hand* concentrates, instead, on oddities: long-lost facts, strange personalities, and unorthodox behaviors that erupted over the course of its nearly 3,000-year history, during which time Etruscans, Oscans, and Sicilians were absorbed by Romans, who, in turn, were sacked and burned by barbarians, then built over by powerful city-states, kingdoms, and the Church, oppressed by a baffling mélange of Austrians, Spanish, French, popes, and anti-popes, and, at last, unified by a bandit from Nice.

"We find the short-haired wool of our speech very unlike the silky and ductile fleece of that of Italy."—Thomas Campbell, *Life and Times of Petrarch,* 1843

"After a first glance into Italian history, the student recoils as from a chaos of inscrutable confusion."—J. A. Symonds, 1888

Organizing this chaos has been anything but simple so, for sanity's sake, I have divided the country geographically, with each chapter focusing on a city or region of particular interest. But the major players in history—Norman conquerors, Renaissance artists, idiosyncratic rulers, writers, and charlatans—had no respect for geography. Neither, ultimately, will this book, for the geography of place matters little compared to the geography of time.

Thus, the stories found in these pages, like those found in any winding street in Italy, defy chronology. In Naples, the pride of place in a 16th-century church goes to a 20th-century saint; his backlit photo in the chapel devoted to him emits a glow far more ethereal than candlelight. From out of the Lombard hinterland, a dirigible sails off to the North Pole; one of its passengers is a sweet terrier named Titina. In catacombs on the outskirts of Palermo, the current concierge, who appears to be in the midst of a typical concierge's nap, has been dead for nearly 200 years. No aspect of Italy is free from this fluidity, neither its Noble Things—its churches, palazzi, art—nor its humbler stuff—its courtesans, gelati, scoundrels.

That my choices have been eclectic, occasionally eccentric, and often bewildering is unavoidable. Italy is a country where there is too much to know, and the sudden awareness of the magnitude of what one doesn't know can be overwhelming. As a result, an important goal of this book is to provide an antidote against Stendhalitis, a condition first identified by the French writer Stendhal (who suffered mightily from it) as sensory overload from too much art, history, heat, noise, and gaiety—even from too many possibilities for love. You'll know you've got it if you find yourself agitated, fainting, and desiring to weep.

The antidote is here, in these pages, in the valuable Italian tradition of *ben trovati*. The original phrase is supposed to go *Se non è vero, è ben trovato* (even if it's not true, it's well invented),[1] a sentiment that could easily apply to the whole country. Italy is a place best understood through its inventions, its legends, and its useful fictions. After all, how can you make sense of a place where its young founders suckled on the milk of wolves? Or a place where coliseums were filled with water in order to hold sea battles in the centers of towns? Or, on a more current note, a place that cherishes scrupulous honesty, except when it comes to bank tellers changing money and waiters padding bills, not to mention double-dealing, tax dodging, moonlighting, and the underground economy. The concept of Italy is at

1 Possibly a *ben trovato* itself.

On the subject of lost and found, don't be alarmed if you are often lost. You're not alone, and should another lost soul ask you for directions, just think of Virgil and Dante, newly arrived in purgatory, and Virgil's answer to such a question: "Why, we're strangers here ourselves!"

once inevitable and absurd; if it existed only in fiction, then only an Italian—a Pirandello, a Fellini, an Eco, or a Calvino—could have invented it, and none of the rest of us would have believed it.

Italy surrounds us in our food, our grand buildings, our history, our books. These beguiling reminders tease us into packing our bags and heading off to this enchanting country, even if only in the imagination. *Italy Out of Hand* is meant to be just such a provocateur.

A note about the type: This book is set in Adobe Bembo, named after the scholar Pietro Bembo, whose essay on Mt Etna, *De Aetna,* was printed in 1495 by Aldus Manutius of Venice (left), using an early Roman type designed by the hotheaded Francesco Griffo da Bologna. Although Griffo is now largely forgotten—he killed his son-in-law during a quarrel and soon after was presumably executed—Aldus Manutius's press became influential, thanks to a revolutionary italic also designed by Griffo. As for Bembo, he became a cardinal and lives on in this classic typeface, refined and reissued by Stanley Morison in 1929.

CAMPOSANTO DI GENOVA

Genova

"[Genoa] is old without antiqueness, narrow without neighbourliness, and ugly beyond all measure."—Heinrich Heine, *Italian Travel Sketches,* c. 1830

Genoa's tough exterior hides its famed and delicate cuisine, the highlight of which is pesto, a sauce of basil, oil, pine nuts, and Parmesan, served on limpid sheets of lasagna or *trenette.* Once you've eaten a good pesto in Genoa, it's easy to forget that any other dishes exist.

PREVIOUS PAGE: *A pamphlet for Genoa's Cimitero di Staglieno, c. 1910.*

IMAGES OF GENOA that come to mind would frighten away all but the fiercest lovers of seediness and chaos. As a Mediterranean port city, it has few equals. It's smelly, noisy, and, in places, menacing, though rarely dangerous. *Vicoli,* narrow lanes, in the old section are towered over by buildings acquainted neither with the concept of right angles nor with the phenomenon of daylight. Prostitutes and pimps hang out in these dark lanes, but they're all over the old part of the city.

Central Genoa is a jumble of legitimate businesses and stuff you don't want to know about. In one small square you can buy fruit and vegetables from motherly types, pastries from gents who wouldn't be out of place in the Savoy, linens from stylish matrons, and hot *telefonini,* cell phones, from men whose faces you should forget. Turn a corner and wonder what kind of trouble you're going to get into; turn another and find yourself on a street of beautiful palazzi.

The contrast between Genoa's airless center and its superb setting is best seen by taking elevators and funiculars up to the incredible vistas of the port and the sea beyond.

You mustn't come to Genoa with expectations of finding "Italy." It's unique, a world apart, to be discovered on its own terms.

6 · GENOVA - Galleria Giuseppe Mazzini

FALSTAFFS

According to rumor, the falstaffs at the Klainguti sustained composer Giuseppe Verdi during his stay in Genoa. This flaky pastry, filled with ground hazelnuts and sugar, seems appropriate for the portly figure of Sir John Falstaff, a character from Shakespeare's *Henry IV* and *The Merry Wives of Windsor* and adopted by Verdi as the subject for his last opera. Verdi's framed testimony, in the form of a note scribbled on a napkin, is on display in the *caffè*.

Nearby is Pietro Romanengo, a 200-year-old *pasticceria*. Just off the Piazza Soziglia, down narrow Via Macelli di Soziglia, are butchers, book and paper workshops, and secondhand shops. A detour shortly after the piazza leads to another, tinier piazza, the former site of a daily flea market (still listed in guidebooks), but at last visit, the number of vendors had dwindled to one.

Gran Caffè Klainguti
Piazza Soziglia 98r

Pietro Romanengo
Via Soziglia 74r

Other distinguished *caffè* and *pasticcerie:*

Mangini
*Piazza Corvetto,
Via Roma 91r,* est. 1876

Adele ved. Romanengo
Via Orefici 31r

Caffè degli Specchi
*Salita Pollaiuoli 43r,
near Palazzo Ducale*

Viganotti
*Vico Castagna 14r,
near Piazza De Ferrari,*
est. 1866

Galleria Mazzini
There are also several decent *caffè* in this 19th-century galleria (above). Just off Via Roma.

A Monumental Cemetery

Sneaking into Genoa's cemetery is just not possible. The keepers of this *camposanto*, holy ground, are keen to ensure that no souls are lost at closing time, so when you enter they will hound you into their office at the gate and implore you to accept a map that can be ignored,

Cimitero di Staglieno
Piazzale Resasco

Revolutionary Vocabulary

Throughout Europe, 1848 was a revolutionary year, and Italy, struggling to throw off Austrian and Bourbon rule, was no exception. Several words came out of this year of uprisings and anarchy:

Quarantottata: rash venture, noisy speeches

Quarantottesco: warlike, swaggering; *fare un quarantotto,* to start pandemonium

Sfrancesarsi: to defrenchify

especially since it can't be followed. In any case, it will not interfere with your appreciation of the magnificent tomb-lined galleries that await you.

These tombs, populated inside and out with granite celestial beings and mortals, are what visitors without interred relatives come to see. The poignant stone angels who comfort the bereaved or whisper into the ears of the departed grab your eyes and wring the tears right out of them. How wise of one of these winged creatures to stop a mourning wife from following her deceased husband into the firmament. How disturbing of another to stand coyly before a slightly open door—is she beckoning you in, or is she letting someone out?

African explorers lie next to lawyers and writers; philosophers slumber beside bureaucrats and accountants. Revolutionaries have been laid to rest next to . . . revolutionaries! The greatest of the lot, Giuseppe Mazzini, a hero of the 1860 Risorgimento, Italy's Resurrection, is here. The epitaph on his tomb reads (according to the translation given on the map): "He gave

his life careless of the ingratitude of the powerful, he was not a plagiarist nor a simulator in the time of slavery."

Ladies, take care in the Galleria Inferiore a Ponente, Lower West Gallery, the first you come to after leaving the helpful and vigilant guards. An elderly gentleman may follow you around; you'll notice that when you stop to read an epitaph, he'll stop. In fact, he may stand awfully close. Is he a Casanova or your personal escort to purgatory? Or does he just want to read what you're reading, in case your eyes have added something of import to the inscriptions that he already knows by heart?

There's also space for English expatriates and for French soldiers, too. Those who visit the section known as the Protestant Cemetery will be interested to know that Oscar Wilde's wife, Constance, lies here. It's been suggested that should she be dug up, the organ missing from the figure on her husband's tomb at Père Lachaise in Paris will also surface.

Istituto Mazziniano: Casa Mazzini, Museo del Risorgimento
Via Lomellini 11

Until 1870, Italy was a collection of distinct states and kingdoms ruled by the Church, by powerful families, or by foreign powers, especially France and Austria. Mazzini, a patriot and a member of the Carbonari[1] (Charcoal burners), a clandestine liberation movement, joined with Garibaldi to unify the country. Mazzini's followers were known as Mazziniani.

1 Lord Byron was an illustrious member of the Carbonari. He joined in 1820, when living in Ravenna.

Leon Battista Alberti

1404–72

Alberti (below), whose family was exiled from Florence, lived in Genoa. He wrote art appreciation and how-to guides, including *Della statua,* on sculpture (facing page), and *De re aedificatoria,* on architecture. His *Della pittura,* on painting, included tips on making dead people look dead. Architect, writer, cartographer, athlete, composer, and mathematician, Alberti was truly a man of the Renaissance.

Art Lesson #1

Certain connoisseurs swear that years of training are necessary to be able to properly appreciate art. But there's really nothing to it, as 19th-century traveler extraordinaire Wilhelmine Buchholz so cleverly demonstrates in the quote from 1887 below. That is, if you have even a modicum of culture in your background.

> If a very fat boy kneels in the foreground with his back turned towards the spectator, then the painting is a genuine Bassano; but if, on the other hand, an utterly shrunken-up old man contemplates a skull with a view to calculating how long [it would take] to become just as thin, you may be sure that it is a St. Hieronymus by Ribera. Ribera frequently paint[ed] a head and one arm only of Hieronymus, spreading a garment over the remainder of the body. He only did this, however, when he was badly paid, as he could not furnish the other arm and legs for the same price.

Further tips include how to recognize "Carlo Dolci by his dilated contours, Raphael by his Madonnas, Titian by the so-called golden tone (which, however, disappears . . . when washed), Michael Angelo by his muscles, &c, &c."

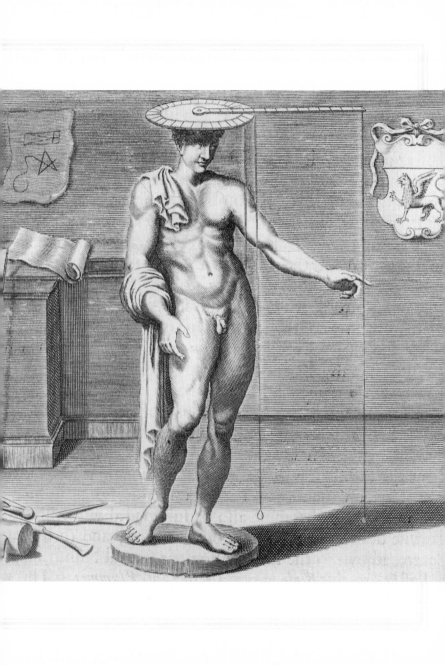

TOP: *Marguerite, Countess of Blessington, 1789–1849.*
BOTTOM: *George Gordon Byron, 6th Baron Byron, 1788–1824.*

BLESSINGTON AND BYRON

In April 1823, wealthy Lady Blessington, an Englishwoman staying in Genoa, met poet Lord Byron for the first time. She was filled with expectation, but was disappointed, finding his nose too thick, his body too thin, and his graying hair over-oiled. His suit fit poorly and looked off the rack. She consoled herself that he was a gentleman bursting with exuberant good humor. Byron, having no expectations at all, was delighted to find her intelligent and beautiful and gladly offered to be her *cicerone,* guide, to Genoa's sights.

Byron lived for nine months in Genoa, in 1823, his last Italian sojourn before his ill-fated mission to Missolonghi, Greece, where he died. He'd come from Pisa after Shelley's tragic drowning and stayed at the Casa Saluzzo, which cost £24 a year. During his seven years in Italy, Byron wrote prolifically, wooed women feverishly, and rode, swam, and traveled tirelessly. He also dieted intemperately, and his weight fluctuated from one end of the scale to the other.

Acquaintances frequently commented on his heft. A friend, meeting him in 1818, wrote that he was "pale, bloated, and sallow. He had grown very fat . . . and the knuckles of his hands were lost in fat." Faithful correspondent Tom Moore commented that, in 1819, Byron's distinctive "refined and spiritualized look" had been submerged. Byron was sensitive about his appearance. He ate very little, at least publicly, limiting his breakfast (taken midafternoon) to a couple of raw eggs, tea, and a biscuit. By the time he met Lady Blessington, he was truly thin and, to her, he extolled his diet, advising abstinence and, above all, avoiding "animal foods."

SPECIALIZED ITALIAN CAREERS

Young men of the 19th century often served no purpose other than mere decoration. The especially pretty ones worked their way into the hearts and beds of countesses and lady tourists alike. The most common of these were the *ciceroni,* guides. Charming, irritating, rapacious, and indispensable to Grand Tourists, they were usually Italian.

The *cavaliere servente* (literally, servant knight) whether Italian, French, German, or British, had a mixed function as a dogsbody with hopes of serving a lady. He would hold her gloves and attend her at the theater. In the words of James Boswell, a young Scot who fell into the job often (even with ladies more than twice his age), the *cavaliere servente* was "a lover without love, a soldier without pay." But Hester Piozzi was convinced that the *cavaliere* "received more favours than he conferred." Every lady

"Nature is all-powerful in Italy, and who is it that would not prefer the sins of her exuberance to the crimes of art?"—Byron, quoted by Lady Blessington, *Conversations with Lord Byron,* 1832

Hester Piozzi
1741–1821
Epistolarian, essayist, and the former Mrs Thrale, Hester lost her close friendship with Samuel Johnson when she married, after Henry Thrale's death, Gabriel Piozzi, an Italian musician. The newlyweds spent 1784 to 1786 touring Italy. She thought Genoa, her second stop in Italy after Turin, a "gaudy city."

Pietro Bembo

1470–1547

Not only a character in *Il cortegiano,* Bembo was the author of *Gli Asolani,* a discourse on love held in the garden of Caterina Cornaro, queen of Cyprus, at Asolo near Venice. It was dedicated to the beautiful Lucrezia Borgia.

had at least one or two. The *bracciere* (from *braccio,* arm), on the other hand, was a temporary stand-in who gave his arm to a lady to escort her to the theater when her busy husband couldn't.

The *cicisbeo,* originally meaning whisperer, was a married lady's lover, recognized by all, even her husband. *Cicisbei* played by set rules, avoiding public displays of affection or usurping the husband's place. Byron was *cicisbeo* to Contessa Teresa Gamba Guiccioli and went so far as to plan to elope with her. After Byron's death, her second husband, Marquis de Boissy, bragged that Byron had been his wife's lover. Boswell, who rivaled Byron in quantities of lovers, became *cicisbeo* to countesses in Turin and Siena.

Former *cavalieri serventi* and *cicisbei* became *spiantati,* cast-offs (literally, penniless, ruined). Stendhal, another energetic *cicisbeo,* was disgusted by women who accepted *spiantati* as lovers.

The *cortigiano,* courtier, was a man of elegance and charm, as exemplified by Baldassare Castiglione, statesman and author of *Il cortegiano* of 1528, conversations on etiquette, chivalry, and learning between some of Italy's leading ladies and gentlemen, including Pietro Bembo.

A Famous Genoan
ANDREA DORIA: 1466–1560

*B*orn into a powerful Genoan family, Andrea Doria became a *condottiere* (mercenary), admiral, and statesman. His ancestors included a long line of naval heroes, one of whom was Branca Doria, thrown into the *Inferno* by Dante for the murder of his father-in-law (Canto 33).

As a *condottiere,* Andrea backed Francis I of France against Holy Roman Emperor Charles V, then, miffed at the low pay, changed sides. He battled continuously and successfully against Turks and Venetians, helped Charles capture Tunis from the infamous pirate Barbarossa, was named Liberator of the Fatherland, and, in gratitude, was given two palazzi, the Doria and the Doria Tursi. Today, Doria Tursi is the Palazzo Municipale, home to Paganini's violin and some of Christopher Columbus's personal papers.

Palazzo Doria
Via Garibaldi 6

Palazzo Doria Tursi
Palazzo Municipale
Via Garibaldi 9

Chiesa di San Matteo
Piazza Matteotti

Pilaster capital from the Palazzo Doria.

Doria was elected *sindacatore,* inspector, to

preside over a senate made up of Genoa's leading families. He died at age 94 and is buried in the family crypt in Genoa's San Matteo (left). With no heirs, the line continued from another branch, becoming the Doria Pamphili.

A Famous Genoan
NICCOLÒ PAGANINI: 1782–1840

"Let my ashes rest in peace."—Niccolò Paganini

A child prodigy and virtuoso violinist, Niccolò Paganini was driven by a passionate and energetic personality. His health was marred by syphilis, causing his face to become gaunt and sallow. As he took mercury to treat the disease, his teeth decayed and fell out, and his chin receded. Yet audiences forgot his macabre appearance when he began to play; his performances were described as sensational. One of his unorthodox techniques was to mistune the violin's strings, a device known as *scordatura;* another was to use one string only. His compositions are difficult for others to play. In 1815, he was tossed into Genoa's Grimaldina Tower, accused of corrupting and abducting a young woman, a charge from which he was eventually absolved.

He died in Nice—of tuberculosis—but was left unburied for a month, because he either refused the last rites or was refused them, and his body could not be accepted in consecrated ground. After he was finally buried, his turbulent corpse was dug up and reinterred several times before it settled at Parma. Even then, he was still not allowed rest; his coffin was opened on occasion, presumably to check that he was still there. His violin, pawned frequently to pay gambling debts, is in Genoa's Palazzo Municipale.

Grimaldina Tower
Palazzo Ducale
Piazza de Ferrari

Silhouette by Albert Edouard, n.d.

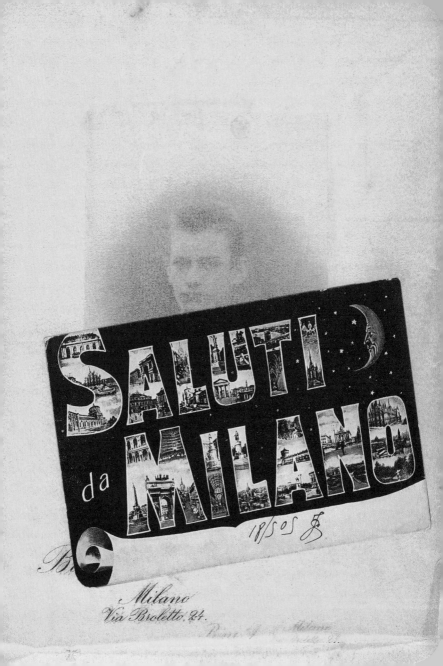

SALUTI da MILANO

18/5 05

Milano
Via Broletto, 24.

Milano

MILAN HAS A PROSPEROUS AND self-absorbed atmosphere. With tall, new buildings and wide, airy streets, not much of Milan could be described as having character. A quick survey of its history will show why.

Milan's fertile location has long attracted a lot of barbarians intent on destroying what came before. Celts, of a tribe known as Insubre, but probably also insalubrious, first settled here in 400 or 500 B.C. They were vanquished by Romans in 222 B.C.

Milan prospered until Huns, in 452, then Goths, in 489 and 539, flattened it. So when Lombards, Germanic barbarians, arrived in 568, no one much cared. Described as vicious and rapacious, the Lombards were wizards at making money and acquiring land. Historian Edward Gibbon called them passionate and, under their brutal exterior, even gentle, unaffected by "the hypocrisy of social manners."

Invasions and pillage continued through years of Holy Roman rule, during control of tyrannical aristocratic families, and into the 19th century when French, Spaniards, and Austrians fought over the city.

Again badly damaged during WWI and II, much of Milan has been rebuilt. But even without many old bits, the stories are there all the same. It just takes more digging to find them.

Milanese: native of Milan

Milanista: supporter of Milan teams

Alla milanese: done the Milan way, or dialect of Milan

Meneghino: Milanese dialect

"[My stay was] like a ship in quarantine."— Byron, 1816

"Retire me to my Milan, where Every third thought shall be my grave."—Shakespeare, *The Tempest*

BACKGROUND: *Milan, 1885.*

LOMBARDIC ORIGINS OF THE FASHION CAPITAL

Milan has been a center of fashion from at least 1530, when the English coined the word *milliner* to mean those Milanese who made ladies' hats.

But the city's rise to its place as the fashion capital of the world may have been a reaction to having been the home of the ugliest barbarians ever. Although the city's founders, the Gauls, weren't noted for their style, the appearance of Germanic plunderers, the Lombards (from Longobard, or Long beard), in 568 provoked ridicule.

Gibbon wrote in *Decline and Fall of the Roman Empire* that they shaved their heads at the back and let "shaggy" hair hang down over their faces, which were adorned with long beards. Their linen outfits were patterned with colorful stripes, and they wore tight, heavy stockings and open sandals. Gibbon also noted that the descendants quickly smartened up and "surveyed with curiosity and affright the portraits of their savage forefathers." As for women's fashion, we have only unreliable portrayals of Queen Theodolinda, made some nine centuries after she died, in the Monza Duomo.

Milanese today have forgotten that they owe thanks to this motley bunch for giving them the incentive to become geniuses of *l'ultima moda*. Would it be cruel to remind them?

Duomo di Monza

Monza, 21 km/13 mi. northeast of Milan

Monza was once famous for its fezzes. Although the fez is no longer made here, other styles of felt hats are still produced.

Fashion Vocabulary

Sfilata di moda: fashion show

Autostrade: freeways, slim girls

Arrivista: parvenu

Farsi vedere: to be seen

Gran mondo: smart set

RULING FAMILIES

Duomo di Milano
Piazza del Duomo

Certosa di Pavia
9 km/5½ mi. north of
Pavia, south of Milan

Bernabò was called
"the Scourge of
Milan" by Chaucer
in *The Monk's Tale*.
Chaucer saw Bernabò
in person when he
visited Milan as a
diplomat in 1378.

Napoleon completed
much of the Duomo's
facade for his corona-
tion. The building has
about 135 spires and
3,500 statues.

FACING PAGE: *Coats of
arms, clockwise from top
left: Visconti, Venice,
unidentified, Anjou, Sforza,
and Ambrosius.*

The Visconti were known as the
Vipers of Milan and not just for their
emblem, an enormous snake swallow-
ing a man. The family's rule began in 1262,
but became especially ill-fated with Matteo I,
who lost his will to live when excommunicated.
His son, Galeazzo I, died in prison; Stefano was
poisoned; Marco was tossed out a window;
Lucchino was poisoned by his wife; Matteo II
shared the rule with two brothers, who stabbed
him. One of those brothers, Bernabò, was stag-
geringly ruthless and fecund; at one point he
had 36 living children and got 18 women,
including his wife, pregnant concurrently. He
died of poison in a dungeon after being
arrested by Gian Galeazzo.

Cultured, cruel, and possibly the most ruthless Visconti, Gian Galeazzo became one of
Italy's mightiest rulers. He was a patron of letters
and arts and began construction of the Duomo
of Milan and the charterhouse, the Certosa
of Pavia. He died of the plague in 1402. His
successor, the sadist Gianmaria, was killed on
his way to church.

The line ended with Filippo-Maria, who
was afraid of thunder and ashamed of his
corpulence. He charged his first wife with
adultery and had her executed once she was
of no further use to him. His second marriage

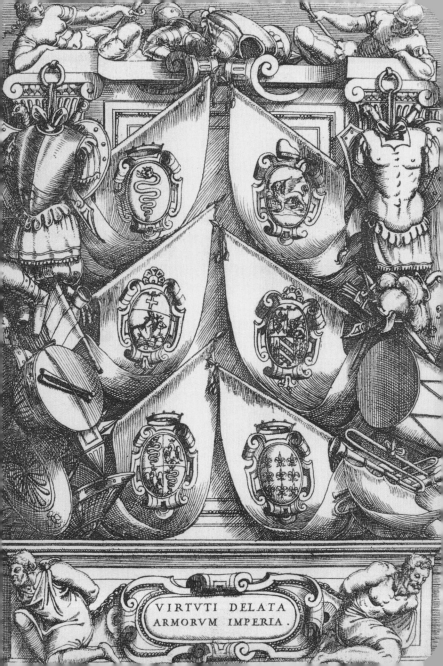

VIRTVTI DELATA
ARMORVM IMPERIA.

Castello Sforzesco
Via Dante,
north end

Ospedale Maggiore
Via dell'Ospedale

Beatrice d'Este
1475–97
Beatrice made the
Sforza court a pleasure
palace. She and
Isabella d'Aragon
played practical jokes
and wore disguises
such as Turkish cos-
tumes. Beatrice was
also a skilled diplomat
and could hold her
own in any court in
Italy. She died in
childbirth.

BACKGROUND: *Leonardo
da Vinci's* The Battle of
the Standard, *about the
victory of the Florentines
over Filippo-Maria Visconti
in 1440.*

went unconsummated when he heard the
baying of a hound at the critical moment. This
poor wife was locked up.

The Visconti gave way in 1450 to the Sforza
(from *sforzare,* to force) when Francesco
Alessandro Sforza, a *condottiere,* mercenary, and
key character in Machiavelli's *The Prince,* married Filippo-Maria's illegitimate child, Bianca
Maria. Milan thrived under him—the imposing
Castello Sforzesco and Ospedale Maggiore
were built during his rule—but sputtered when
his son, Galeazzo Maria, took over in 1476. A
well-placed thrust of a dagger put an end to
him ten years later. His son, Gian Galeazzo,
married Isabella d'Aragon, daughter of the King
of Naples. Two years after he came to power, he
died, perhaps at the hand of his uncle, Lodovico
Maria Sforza, *il Moro,* the Moor.

Lodovico was a patron of the arts and an
early industrialist. He married Beatrice d'Este
from the equally brilliant court of Ferrara and
had a reputation for tinting his hair. His trust
in France's Charles VIII, who died from an
untimely blow to the head at a tennis game,
led to the fall of the Sforza and to the estab-
lishment of foreign rule in Lombardy when his
enemy, Louis XII, took the throne. Lodovico
fled Milan in 1499 but was caught and spent
the rest of his life in a French prison. He died
in 1508.

THE LAST SUPPER

Great artist, engineer, architect, anatomist, and inventor Leonardo da Vinci was employed in the 1490s as Lodovico Sforza's *pictor et ingeniarius ducalis* (the duke's painter and engineer). Sforza kept Leonardo busy with Milan's great cathedral, the Duomo (begun in 1386 by Gian Galeazzo Visconti and not completed until the end of the 19th century). The artist also entertained the court with his lyre.

His *Il Cenacolo, The Last Supper,* at Santa Maria delle Grazie, nearly became *The Lost Supper.* The fresco was damaged by smoke, a door was cut into it, it was overpainted, then carelessly restored, then Napoleon's soldiers vandalized it. But its dreadful state owes more to the fact that Leonardo was experimenting when he painted it. Impatient with the technique of applying tempera onto wet plaster, he painted onto dry plaster, which began to self-destruct soon after. These days, in order to view it, you need to make reservations and pass through depollution chambers.

Santa Maria delle Grazie
Piazza Santa Maria delle Grazie

Casa Conti
Corso Magenta 65–67, near Santa Maria delle Grazie
Leonardo was born in Vinci, near Florence, and died at Cloux, near Amboise, in France. The Casa degli Atellani, now part of Casa Conti, was his home in Milan.

Leonardesco: in the manner of Leonardo

Biblioteca Ambrosiana

Palazzo Ambrosiano

Piazza Pio XI

Byron, a romantic souvenir hunter, also took a couple of pieces of granite from Juliet's tomb in Verona.

"Borgia, thou once were almost too august,
And high for adoration—now thou'rt dust!
All that remains of thee these plaits infold
Calm hair, meand'ring with pellucid gold!"
—Walter Savage Landor

BACKGROUND: *A portion of one of Bembo's poems to Lucrezia Borgia, on the subject of her golden hair.*

AMBROSIANA LIBRARY

It is assumed that this renowned library, founded by Cardinal Federico Borromeo in 1609, was named after St Ambrose, a bishop who scattered his name all over Milan, but the distinctive and not unpleasant odor permeating the building suggests an alternative origin. Dante's line from *Purgatorio,* "With such an odour as ambrosia has," hints at a fragrant interpretation. In keeping with the olfactory theme, the *pinacoteca,* art gallery, houses Caravaggio's *Basket of Fruit* and Brueghel's *Mouse with a Rose.*

Lady Mary Wortley Montagu in 1739 and Byron in 1816, among others, were given free access to the library's treasures. But when Mary Shelley visited in 1840, patrons were closely watched. The librarians were concerned about theft, having recently suffered an attempt on Petrarch's annotated *Virgil,* and no doubt they had heard that Byron, taken with the memory of Lucrezia Borgia, had stolen a strand of her blonde hair from a lock squirreled away in their collection of her letters to Pietro Bembo. The strand was reputedly passed along to English writer Leigh Hunt. In 1825, Hunt showed it to Walter Savage Landor, who penned a few lines in its honor. The strand's trail goes cold here, but the original plait is now in a reliquary on display in the museum.

A Famous Milanese
ALESSANDRO MANZONI: 1785–1873

"How a trifle is sometimes enough to decide a man's fate for life!"
—Alessandro Manzoni, *The Betrothed*

Manzoni's epic novel *I promessi sposi, The Betrothed* (1827), was set in the 17th-century Lombard countryside and in Milan. It was rewritten twice, the last edition appearing in 1840. The final version, in Tuscan Italian, was instrumental in creating a common Italian language that prevailed over the many local dialects. When the novel was first published, it was to immediate acclaim, selling some 600 copies in 20 days. But it was controversial, too. Its hero and heroine were peasants, which some found inspiring, others, incomprehensible. The story was regarded as either overtly religious or immoral and the writing enchanting or mediocre. In Rome, sales of *The Betrothed* were halted, as it was seen as an attack on monastic orders. The book quickly attracted international attention, thanks to the praise of Goethe and others, and has been compared with the novels of Tolstoy, Dickens, and Scott. It's still required reading in Italian schools; efforts to update the curriculum by removing it have been met with outrage. The Manzoni Library, in the writer's house, has almost all of the 500 editions ever published, as well as illustrations, documents, and Manzoni memorabilia. Manzoni lived here from 1814 to his death in 1873.

His death was deeply mourned and, fittingly, another resident of Milan, Giuseppe Verdi, composed the requiem for his funeral.

Centro Nazionale di Studi Manzoniani
Casa del Manzoni
Via Morone 1,
near Piazza della Scala

Teatro alla Scala

Piazza della Scala

Stendhal's book *Rome, Naples and Florence* should have been called *Milan, Bologna and a Couple of Other Cities.* The author, a dawdler, doesn't even arrive at the first of his haphazardly listed cities, Florence, until more than halfway through the book.

"Dare I say what moved me the most upon arriving at Milan? It's obvious that this is written for no one but myself. It was a certain smell of manure peculiar to its streets."—Stendhal, 1811

LA SCALA AND STENDHAL

Few could claim a more thorough knowledge of Milan's Teatro alla Scala than the French writer Stendhal (Marie-Henri Beyle). Living in Milan in 1811, he attended performances at La Scala almost every night. There he met other visitors, such as Lord Byron, planned assignations, and sharpened his commentary on Milanese society, with which he was intimate. He received his mistress Angela Pietragrua at his lodgings in the Contrada de' Due Muri, Street of the Two Walls, not far from the theater.

La Scala, which means ladder or staircase,[1] was situated on the former site of Santa Maria della Scala, a church that had been built for the Scalas, descendants of the wealthy Veronese Scaligeri family. The theater, which replaced an earlier one that had burned down in 1776, was designed by Giuseppe Piermarini and opened in 1778 with *Europa riconosciuta* by Antonio Salieri, a spectacle filled with storms at sea, shipwreck, lightning, and 36 horses. Other notable premieres were Verdi's first and last operas, *Oberto* and *Falstaff* (and many in between), Rossini's *La gazza ladra,* Donizetti's *Lucrezia Borgia,* and Bellini's *Norma.* After being destroyed by bombs in 1943, La Scala was rebuilt and reopened in 1946.

1 *Scala* in Lombardian means goblet. Alboin, the king of the Lombards, had one made from the skull of an enemy.

GIUSEPPE VERDI

Verdi was a prolific composer, creating some 27 operas, including *Rigoletto, La traviata, Otello, Falstaff, Nabucco* (which featured the aria that became the anthem of the Risorgimento), and *Aïda,* the grandest grand opera of them all. He was encouraged from an early age by mentors who clearly recognized his potential genius. Many of his highly dramatic operas were presented at La Scala and, for the most part, were received with great enthusiasm.

Folks in his hometown of Le Roncole disapproved of him living openly with his mistress, singer Giuseppina Strepponi, whom he later married. After her death in 1897, Verdi lived in the Milano Grand Hotel. When he died in 1901, the quarter-million mourners that lined Milan's streets spontaneously sang the famed anthem from *Nabucco.* He is buried at the *Casa di Riposo per Musicisti* in west Milan, the musicians' retirement home that his royalties had funded until the copyrights on his operas expired.

Grand Hotel et de Milan
Via Manzoni 29

Casa di Riposo per Musicisti
Piazza Buonarroti

Vocabolario musicale:
Bel canto: highly ornamented singing
Cantilena: long, fluid melody
Canzone: ballad
Canzonetta: short or comic song
Intermezzo: interlude, often a comic play or ballet
Opera buffa: comic opera
Opera giocosa: comic opera with serious bits

Caffè Zucca

Piazza del Duomo 21
In business for more
than 100 years, the
Zucca was briefly
known as the Campari,
or Camparino, after its
creation, the Campari
aperitif. Patrons
included Toscanini
and Verdi.

Cova

Via Monte Napoleone 8
Founded in 1817 and
now a *pasticceria* and
confetteria.

Pasticceria Taveggia

*Via Visconti di
Modrone 2*
Est. early 1900s.

Caffè Biffi della Scala

One of the original
tenants of Milan's
extravagant Galleria
Vittorio Emanuele.

CAFFÈ

Italian coffees are based on strong
espresso, usually three or four sips'
worth. The first patent registered for the steam
espresso machine was in Milan, by Luigi
Bezzera in 1903. Depending on whom you
read, Desiderio Pavoni invented the machine
or he bought the patent from Bezzera in 1905.
In any case, Pavoni manufactured the machine,
and it was soon found all over Europe.

Chances are that the espresso you take at
one of Milan's historic *caffè* will be dripped
from one of Pavoni's machines.

Cappuccino: only served after 10 AM to children
and tourists
Caffè latte: cappuccino with little or no foam
and more milk
Corretto: "corrected" with grappa or brandy
Caffè freddo: cold coffee
Hag: a brand name, used to mean decaffeinated
coffee
Lungo: diluted espresso
Macchiato: "stained" with steamed milk;
also slang for repeat offender
Marocchino: cappuccino with less milk
Ristretto: extra-strong espresso
Schiuma: the dense foam that forms on the
surface of espresso

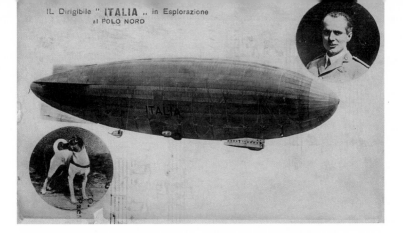
IL Dirigibile " ITALIA ,, in Esplorazione al POLO NORD

NOBILE AND TITINA

In 1928, Milanese General Umberto Nobile flew his dirigible, *Italia,* to the North Pole with a crew of 18 and his fox terrier Titina. It was his second attempt to explore the Arctic by airship. The first, two years earlier, was deemed successful, and Nobile returned a hero, even though his dirigible, *Norge,* was badly damaged.

The *Italia* left Milan on 28 April, with the blessing of Benito Mussolini, who savored the anticipated prestige the expedition would bring him. Assisted by a multinational crew of engineers and explorers, Nobile dropped the Italian flag at the North Pole. The return journey, however, ended disastrously when the dirigible crashed, disgorged some of the crew onto the ice, then took off again with six still aboard. Nobile and Titina survived, but Nobile was accused of treason by a livid Mussolini. He emigrated, first to the Soviet Union, then to the United States. He returned to Italy in 1945.

The Red Tent

This Italian/Soviet film about the doomed *Italia* was made in 1970. In it, Nobile, played by Peter Finch, calls together the dead members of his crew to relive their frigid nightmare. It also starred Sean Connery and Claudia Cardinale.

PNF DOPOLAVORO OND
FORZE ARMATE

Piazzale Loreto
*North end of Corso
Buenos Aires, east of the
Stazione Centrale,
Central Train Station*

"[Mussolini] was
practically defeated by
one man alone, him-
self."—Luigi Barzini,
The Italians

BENITO MUSSOLINI

Mussolini, known as Il Duce,
began and ended his political
career in Milan. A one-time
socialist and editor of the socialist
journal *Avanti*, he organized a
meeting in Milan, on 23 March
1919, to form Fasci Italiani di
Combattimento (Italian Leagues of
Combat). Made up of a disparate
group of malcontents, including
rabid nationalists and the unem-
ployed, the Fasci officially targeted
communists and socialists, especially in the north. But democracy
was another casualty: in 1921, Italy
held its last free election for 25 years.

Mussolini's reign was one of terror. He took
Italy into WWII, allied with Hitler, and held on
until 1945, when the Allies succeeded in breaking Italy's resistance. Mussolini fled, intending
to take his family and his mistress, Clara Petacci,
to Switzerland.

Mussolini and Petacci were caught and
executed on 28 April 1945, then hung up on
display at Milan's Piazzale Loreto. This otherwise unremarkable and busy square has none
of the grandeur of Rome's Fascist buildings,
but it is a grim reminder of a not-so-distant
barbarian past.

SCIOPERI

Chances are you'll be caught up in a *sciopero,* strike, if you spend any time in Italy. It may be only a slowdown, it may last for a day, or it may be a full-scale halt. Most are minor inconveniences, not like the general strike of 1898, which left 81 dead and 502 injured. The strikes at the turn of the last century were unparalleled in their frequency and violence. In 1899, there were 678; in 1901, the number rose to 2,707. Labor unrest was suppressed under Fascism until 1943.

Gladiators held what may have been the first strike, in 73 B.C. Led by Spartacus from Thrace, the gladiators protested their living conditions and for two years confronted waves of Roman legionnaires. When they were finally overcome, retribution was harsh; Spartacus and his 6,000 followers were crucified. Their bodies lined the Appian Way, a warning to other would-be rebels.

A strike in Italy today is commonplace— from the guys who deliver money to banks to attendants of autostrada rest area washrooms— but landmark strikes still occur. In 2002, McDonald's was hit by its first strike. The first general strike in 20 years was also called that year. It was supported by an estimated 10 million workers belonging to trade unions with an array of confusing acronyms such as the GGIL, UIL, CISL, COBAS, CUB, and RdB.

Vocabolario sciopero

Frenare la produzione: to slow down

Scioperaggine: laziness

Scioperante: striker, on strike

Scioperare: to go on strike

BACKGROUND: *A Thracian gladiator.*

Excursion from Milan: Locate
CRISTINA BARBIANO DI BELGIOJOSO: 1808–71

The villa of *principessa* Cristina di Belgiojoso at Locate, south of Milan, was the site of an unusual memento mori. While the beautiful but haunted princess—who lived only sporadically at Locate—was nursing rebels in Rome in 1848, secret police employed by the Austrians were searching the villa, looking for documents that might justify her arrest.

They found, instead, the corpse of her beloved secretary, Gaetano Stelzi, who had died of consumption the year before, inside a wardrobe. When they disinterred the coffin that should have held his body, they found only a log.

According to one rumor, Belgiojoso and her English maid, Mrs Parker, had embalmed Stelzi's body in the kitchen, then dressed him up and hid him. Before the police could grab them, Belgiojoso, Parker, and Maria, Belgiojoso's daughter, escaped on a ship bound for Constantinople.

Safely in Turkey, Belgiojoso bought a farm near the Black Sea and cultivated poppies. After a successful opium harvest, she headed south on horseback for a 10-month tour of Syria and the Holy Land.

Before her Levant sojourn, Belgiojoso had lived in self-exile in Paris from 1831, but returned to Milan in 1847, when the Austrians were briefly expelled. When they reestablished themselves, she led a force into Milan in an unsuccessful takeover attempt. In Rome, she formed a corps of military nurses, recruiting local and foreign women, including the American Margaret Fuller, who became Countess Ossoli.

Villa Trivuliziano
Locate,
16 km/10 mi. south
of Milan

Bologna

"First, we went to the cathedral, which contains nothing remarkable, except a kind of shrine . . . loaded with sculptures, and supported on four marble columns. We went then to a palace—I am sure I forget the name of it—where we saw a large gallery of pictures. Of course, in a picture gallery you see three hundred pictures you forget, for one you remember."
—Shelley, 1818

"I am at length joined to Bologna, where I am settled like a sausage."—Byron, 1819

PREVIOUS PAGE: *Tourist brochure for Emilia-Romagna, c. 1930. Signed "Campi."*

ON A COLD WET DAY, Bologna, built of monotone red brick, can seem forbiddingly austere and empty. The city's medieval atmosphere is emphasized by arcades incorporated into most buildings, which are godsends in any kind of weather. As you dash from one arcade to the next to avoid getting soaked or fried, the impression of solitude overwhelms, and even on bright, sunny days, you may ask yourself, "Where is everyone?"

Most earlier visitors just passed through. Boswell, in 1765, not finding any countesses to bed, jammed in some sightseeing. Twenty years later, Hester Piozzi stayed just long enough to conclude that the Bolognese were too pious, having thoughts only for the next world. She may have misunderstood them, as she reviled their accent. And Goethe rushed through so fast in 1786 that he wrote, "I don't know if I drove out of Bologna today or was driven out." Those who did stay for any length of time included the chronically ill poet Giacomo Leopardi, who froze during his residence in 1825. He became so thin and sick he called himself a "walking sepulchre."

The real life of the city is the university. It's only a short hop from the center to this lively quarter, and once you've been there, you'll see how it dominates Bologna's life and history.

L'UNIVERSITÀ

The best way to comprehend the scope of Bologna's university is to visit its many museums, spread out over a large area and almost totally devoted to medicine and science. Anatomy is especially well represented and offers amazing insight not only into the composition of the body but also into how the body was viewed by early anatomists.

The Museum of Human Anatomy[1] was established in 1907 in a building founded in 1742 by Bolognese pope Benedict XIV as an anatomy theater. The museum's collection of 18th-century wax anatomical models was created by Ercole Maria Lelli and Anna Morandi Manzolini and her husband, Giovanni.

Lelli made the eight full-height anatomical statues. The Manzolinis—themselves vividly portrayed at the museum in wax—created many of the detailed sculptures, including a series showing the movements of the eye and a fetus attached to the placenta. One of the fetus's tiny hands delicately holds back the skin of the belly to reveal the inner organs.

1 Bologna University's other anatomical museums include Museo Ostetrico (obstetrics), Palazzo Poggi, Via Zamboni 33; Museo di Anatomia Comparata (comparative anatomy), Via Selmi 3; Museo di Anatomia Patologica (pathology) and Museo Anatomica di Animali Domestici (domesticated animals), Via Tolara di Sopra 50; and Museo Cesare Taruffi, Via Massarenti 9.

Museo di Anatomia Umana Normale

Via Irnerio 48

Remarkable but lost anatomical specimens Brigitta Giorgi Banti (1759–1806), a brilliant, untrained soprano, who sang in operas by Gluck, bequeathed her larynx (presumed lost) to Bologna.

A Famous Anatomist
JACOPO BERENGARIO DA CARPI: c. 1470–1530

*B*erengario da Carpi, a professor of anatomy at Bologna, published a series of anatomical figures—skeletons and flayed musclemen—in 1521. Though crude, they were a dramatic and brave attempt to peel away the layers of the body and educate other physicians. His work is considered a forerunner to that of Andreas Vesalius, the great Flemish anatomist.

Berengario's methods of dissection may have been dire: he is rumored to have cut up two living Spaniards. He claimed to have dissected several hundred bodies, a remarkable feat for a time when dissection was considered an offence against God. Aside from the occasional criminal's cadaver thrown their way, anatomists needed cunning and courage to get their hands on human specimens.

Mikrokosmographia, or A Description of the Body of Man: Being a Practical Anatomy Shewing the Manner of Anatomizing from Part to Part, The Like Hath not Been set Forth in the English Tongue, Adorned with Many Demonstrative Figures —The title of the 1664 English edition of Berengario's book on anatomy

The artist Benvenuto Cellini, in his autobiography, noted that Berengario was an art connoisseur and owned Raphael's *John the Baptist.* Cellini had firsthand experience of Berengario's hard-nosed business practices when he was treated for what he called "a certain disease . . . that was extremely prevalent among the priests." He complained that Berengario insisted on prepayment for his surefire cure *before* embarking on treatment. The cure was presumably well worth the cost, as Cellini wrote no further of this particular affliction.

CABINETS OF CURIOSITIES

The cabinet of curiosity, commonly known by the German *wunderkammer,* was a personal museum as well as a philosophical endeavor that aimed to construct a systematic approach to understanding nature and humankind's place in it. It was also a fascinating receptacle of the world's odd objects and beliefs. Cabinet owners were driven to collect by curiosity. Some catalogued their accumulations, and all welcomed visitors, especially potential patrons or donors. Collections consisted of the ordinary—minerals, shells, plants, books, and insects—and such exotic rarities as pygmies, crocodiles, coral, papyri, birds of paradise, and unicorn horns. The first *wunderkammern* were started in the 16th century and became most popular in the 17th.

There were *gabinetti fisici* throughout Italy, notably Ferrante Imperato's in Naples and Athanasius Kircher's in Rome, but among the greatest was that of Ulisse Aldrovandi in Bologna. This

The Ravenna Monster (background) was one of the various monsters popular at the beginning of the 16th century. It had a human head and torso, wings for arms, a unicorn's horn, scaly haunches meeting in a single three-toed claw, and an eye where the knee would be. This and other monsters were featured in *Monstrorum historia* by Ulisse Aldrovandi, published posthumously in 1658.

Bologna's other odd and wonderful university museums:

Musei di Architettura Militare, delle Navi, e di Astronomia
(military architecture, navy, and astronomy)
Via Zamboni 33

Musei di Geologia e Paleontologia e Diluviano
(geology and paleontology, and flood)
Via Zamboni 63

Museo di Fisica (physics)
Via Irnerio 46

Museo di Mineralogia
(mineralogy)
Piazza di Porta San Donato 1

Musei di Antropologia e di Zoologia (anthropology and zoology)
Via Selmi 3

museum attracted the attention of European scholars, both academic and ecclesiastical. By 1600 the number of objects in his collection had grown to 20,000 and included a dragon that had appeared in 1572, just before Gregory XIII's investiture as pope. Aldrovandi classified it as *Dragone mostroficato* and featured it in *Dracologia* (1639). The appearance of the dragon was a bad omen for Gregory, but Aldrovandi profited from it.

Aldrovandi bequeathed his collection to Bologna on the condition that his work be published posthumously. The process was so slow, and his accumulated material so extensive, that the executors gave up before they'd exhausted his writings, which had become terribly out-of-date. What remains of his collection today consists mostly of papers and books, now part of the university's library.

GALVANISM

Bologna produced three important scientists in the field of electricity. The most recent, Guglielmo Marconi, became a household name as the father of radio, but few recall Luigi Galvani, after whom the word *galvanism* was coined, and no one remembers Laura Bassi.

Galvani (1737–98) was a scientist, lecturer, and early experimenter with electricity. He observed that certain metals caused convulsions in the legs of dead frogs, though one source suggested that his wife made the discovery while preparing dinner. He published his results in his book *De viribus electricitatis in motu musculari commentarius.*

Bassi (1711–78) was a Latin and philosophy scholar, a lecturer on anatomy, and an experimenter in physics and electricity (preceding Galvani and Volta by several decades). Although not the first woman to obtain a university doctorate degree (that honor had been taken by Elena Lucrezia Cornaro-Piscopia a century earlier), she was the first to teach at a European university, having joined the Bologna faculty at the age of 21. The author of numerous papers on mechanics, chemistry, mathematics, physics, and hydraulics, she was also respected for bringing Newton's theories to Italy. She somehow found the time to have 12 children.

Museo Marconi
Museum of the History of Radio
Fondazione Guglielmo Marconi
Villa Griffone
Via Celestini 1
Pontecchio Marconi,
14 km/9 mi. south of Bologna

Galvani's House
Via Ugo Bassi

Galvani's statue
Piazza Galvani

Alessandro Volta
1745–1827
Volta of Pavia gave his name to the word *voltage.*

Gregory XIII

Pope: 1572–85
Before becoming
pope, Gregory had an
illegitimate son and
was nepotistic but
after election led a
spotless personal life.
As pope, he was well
regarded for promoting
missionary activities,
completing Rome's
Il Gesù church, and
founding colleges.
On the other hand,
he was a counter-
reformationist, praised
the St Bartholomew
Day massacre, sup-
ported plans to assassi-
nate Elizabeth I, and
appropriated lands to
solve his perpetual
need for money.

Basilica di San Petronio
Via dell'Archiginnasio

BOLOGNA TIME

Pope Gregory XIII, originally
Ugo Buoncampagni from Bologna,
replaced the Julian calendar with
the Gregorian in 1582, based on
experiments with time done in
Bologna. Italy (except Florence and
Pisa, which changed in 1749), Poland,
Spain, and Portugal were the first countries to
adopt the new calendar. Their citizens went to
bed on October 4th and woke up on the 15th.
The result was predictable: wages, birthdays,
and interest on loans were lost; confused and
angry citizens demanded the restoration of
their 10 missing days.

Out of spite, non-Catholic countries delayed
their acceptance of the new system. Great
Britain, for example, adopted it in 1752. Russia
changed in 1918, and by then was obliged to
eliminate 13 days. The Orthodox Church still
follows the Julian calendar.

Bologna's Basilica di San Petronio pays
homage to the city's connection with time by
housing an astronomical clock designed in
1655 by Giovanni Domenico Cassini, a professor of astronomy at Bologna. A meridian
marker on the floor coincides with an aperture
in the vaulting and indicates solar noon. It can
also tell the date by the length of the shadow
cast on it.

Excursion from Bologna: Modena

*M*odena, 40 km/24 mi. west of Bologna, is well known for its *aceto balsamico,* balsamic vinegar aged in a succession of barrels of differing woods. Composer Gioacchino Rossini claimed that the vinegar cured him of scurvy. Modena's other specialty, *zamponi,* big paws, has yet to attain such fame. Consisting of deboned pig's trotters stuffed with minced pork, nutmeg, cinnamon, and cloves, *zamponi* are cooked for hours, then served sliced. Rossini, a gourmand in both reputation and physique, craved *zamponi* so much while in Paris that he sent away for some, as did Giuseppe Mazzini in faraway London.

Another Modena highlight is the bucket in the Torre La Ghirlandina, Little Garland Tower. This bucket, filched by marauding Modenans for no apparent reason in 1325, is still displayed, offering the same degree of sustenance to the imagination that it did in 1844 for Charles Dickens, who wrote of it in *Pictures from Italy:*

Torre La Ghirlandina
Piazza Grande

"If ever you should come to Modena, (Where, among other relics, you may see Tassoni's bucket—but 'tis not the true one) Stop at a palace near the Reggio Gate."
—Samuel Rogers, sowing doubt on the bucket's authenticity

I made no effort to see the bucket . . . which the people of Modena took away from the people of Bologna in the fourteenth century, about which there was war made and a mock-heroic poem by Tassoni, too.[2] Being quite content, however, to look at the outside of the Tower, and feast, in imagination, on the bucket within; and preferring to loiter in the shade of the tall Campanile, and about the Cathedral; I have no personal knowledge of this bucket, even at the present time.

2 Alessandro Tassoni, *La secchia rapita, The Rape of the Bucket,* 1622

Excursion from Bologna: Parma

Parma is just far enough from Bologna that it may be worth staying the night, but keep in mind that your first view of the prosperous city may be of other travelers looking for accommodation. A good deal of time is spent despairing over hotels closed for the season, for repair, or for no reason at all. The alternatives are to pay dearly for a room at an upscale hotel or to arrive early, stay the day, and sleep elsewhere.

It would be a shame to pass over this beautiful city even though, on the surface, there doesn't seem to be much to see or do—and what you have associated with Parma may be a fiction. The center for prosciutto, the famed Parma ham, is actually Langhirano, south of the city; Parmesan cheese comes from nearby Reggio Emilia, hence the label Parmigiano-Reggiano; Parma violets, once a thriving industry promoted by Duchess of Parma, Marie-Louise, no longer exist except in plastic. Fortunately, for those counting on Stendhal's novel of the same name, there *is* a charterhouse, *certosa,* of Parma.

But the Duomo alone is worth the stop, for it is, like several other buildings in Parma, awash with glorious frescoes by Antonio Allegri da Correggio.

According to biographer Giorgio Vasari, Mannerist painter Correggio was melancholic and timid. But he didn't hold back exuberance

Improsciuttire: to grow old and withered

Marie-Louise Bonaparte
1791–1847
Marie-Louise was Napoleon's second wife and the Duchess of Parma from 1814 until 1847. While Napoleon was exiled on Elba, she ruled Parma with her one-eyed lover, dashing Count von Neipperg.

Certosa di Parma
Via Mantova
4 km/2½ mi. east of Parma's center

FACING PAGE: *From the Convent of San Paolo, Parma,* Boy Blowing a Shell, *by Correggio.*

Convento di San Paolo
Camera di San Paolo
Via Melloni

Chiesa di San Giovanni Evangelista
Piazzale San Giovanni

Duomo
Piazza del Duomo

Museo Bodoniano
Piazza della Pilotta 5
By appointment,
tel. 0521 220 411

Bodoniano: in the way
of Bodoni

when it came to his work in Parma. The stunning colors, remarkable use of space and modeling, and imaginative foreshortening are features of his frescoes in the Convent of San Paolo (mythological scenes), in San Giovanni Evangelista (*Vision of St John,* the dome), and in the Duomo, Parma's cathedral (*Assumption of the Virgin,* the dome).

Correggio was reputed to be chronically underpaid, and for one of his last commissions, he was compensated with the equivalent of 50 scudi, in small coin. In a fit of parsimony, he walked home with the heavy load, in spite of the great heat that day. He became ill from fever and died, at age 40.

Giambattista Bodoni was another famous Parma resident. A celebrated printer and type founder, he first worked in Rome as a typesetter for the Propaganda Fide, a body of cardinals who organized missionary activities. Then in 1768, he was asked to run the Duke of Parma's royal press.

Bodoni became a stop on the Grand Tour, attracting visitors such as Stendhal, who admired the beauty of his books. Known as a perfectionist, Bodoni admitted to Stendhal that he'd spent six months laboring over the typeface for one book. An incredulous Stendhal wrote, "to such lengths of absurdity may our passions lead us." Bodoni's meticulousness apparently didn't extend to proofreading; the number of errors in his English edition of Horace Walpole's *Castle of Otranto* nearly made the author tear his hair out.

FERRARA

"MY PEN WAS JUST upon the point of praising [Ferrara's] cleanliness . . . till I reflected there was nobody to dirty it." So wrote Hester Piozzi in 1785, and one can say much the same thing today.

Ferrara's quiet gives you a chance to reflect on the Este family, who governed from the mid-900s until 1597, first as head magistrates, then as hereditary princes, and how ripe the city is with their past intrigues. During their rule, for example, Nicolò III murdered his wife, Parisina, and her lover, his illegitimate son, Ugo. Nicolò was probably poisoned. Ercole I tried to poison a nephew.

Yet the Estes, especially Ercole and Alfonso I, held a brilliant court. They were patrons of Ariosto, Titian, and Tasso. Ercole I invited Sephardic Jews exiled from Spain to the city, establishing an atmosphere of tolerance rare for the time. The brilliance is evident still, apparent in its superb palaces. The imposing Castello Estense, with its austere exterior and sumptuous interior, was built in 1385 and became the ducal palace. The Palazzo Schifanoia (the name comes from *schivare la noia,* flee boredom) was built as a pleasure palace. And Palazzina di Marfisa d'Este became home to a lustful ghost.

As many stories circulated about Marfisa d'Este, daughter of Francesco d'Este, as about her grandmother, Lucrezia Borgia. Gossips told

Two statues of Estes, one of Nicolò III, the other of Borso, at the entrance to the cathedral, are replicas. Napoleon melted down the originals to make cannons.

Castello Estense
Piazza Castello

Palazzo Schifanoia
Civic Museum of Ancient Art
Via Scandiana 23

PREVIOUS PAGE: *View of Ferrara and the Castello Estense, c. 1859.*
BACKGROUND: *Castello Estense, c. 1890.*

49

of her nocturnal hunts for lovers, who were murdered after one short, passionate night. So bad was her reputation that, after her death in 1608, an eerie green glow was said to light up her *palazzina,* and her ghost was seen haunting the place. Sober history intervenes and offers, instead, a more likely picture of an independent woman who bucked convention.

Lucrezia Borgia, "the gifted toxicologist," was the illegitimate daughter of Alexander VI (the second Borgia pope), and sister of the ruthless Cesare, who benefited greatly from his father's celebrated nepotism. Lucrezia married into the Sforza dynasty at the age of 13, but her father annulled the marriage on grounds of nonconsumation (in spite of a reputed baby), when he saw a better alliance elsewhere. The next marriage, to a son of the Aragonese ruler of Naples, ended when the young husband was strangled, presumably on Alexander VI's orders. Her third, and last, marriage was to Alfonso I d'Este.

Lucrezia supposedly gave poisonous little suppers to enemies of the Borgias, and this deadly reputation was buttressed by Victor Hugo's lively tale, *Lucrèce Borgia.* In truth, the worst thing that can be said about her is that she was vainly proud of her long, golden locks. Lucrezia died of childbirth complications. She is buried at Ferrara's Convent of Corpus Domini.

Palazzina di Marfisa d'Este
Corso della Giovecca 170

Lucrèce Borgia
In his 1833 play about Lucrezia, Victor Hugo paints the duchess as a tempestuous woman who learned violence and vengence from her corrupt family. In Act I, when warned to disguise herself so her enemies won't recognize her, she replies, "What do I care? If they don't know who I am, I have nothing to fear. If they do know who I am, then it's they who should be fearful."

Convento di Corpus Domini
Via Campofranco

Tasso was born in
Sorrento. For cen-
turies, visitors could
stay in his house,
which had been
incorporated into the
Hotel Tasso, until it
slipped into the sea
sometime after 1840.

FERRARA'S COURT POETS

The Estes were patrons of two poets in particular, Ludovico Ariosto, best known for *Orlando
furioso,* a mythic poem about chivalrous
knights and ladies, and Torquato Tasso, the
author of the epic poem of the First Crusades,
Gerusalemme liberata, Jerusalem Delivered.

Tasso's life is especially interesting because
of an unfortunate downturn in his luck when
he asked the foremost poets of the time what
they thought of his *Gerusalemme.* They loved it,
they declared, but could he add more romance
or consider the Inquisition's reaction? The
criticisms, combined with overwork, broke his
health; he grew suspicious and deluded, then
after a quarrel during which he drew a knife,
he was locked up. For seven years he lan-
guished in a squalid cell, which came to be
known as "Tasso's Prison." Marfisa d'Este may
have helped him escape. Who imprisoned him
or if the story is even true is uncertain.

In 1595, he was invited to Rome to accept
the poet laureate's crown, but he died before
the ceremony took place. His tomb is in Rome
at the Convento di Sant'Onofrio, near St Peter's.

His prison attracted many visitors, including
Byron, who reputedly locked himself in for
several hours, hoping for inspiration. Shelley,
who called Tasso "the world's rejected guest,"
stole a sliver of wood from the door.

Excursion from Ferrara: Ravenna

*M*ost people go to Ravenna for the Byzantine mosaics or as a stop on their way to one of the nearby Adriatic resorts. Some may go because other cities are full, a lucky chance to visit one of Italy's truly pleasant places.

Ravenna has an illustrious past—as an important Roman harbor, then as the Empire's capital from about 400 until its fall in 472. But by the time Humphrey Davy, the chemical scientist, visited in 1820, it had a reputation of being dull, and he thought it rather "savage." Not even Byron, who lived there with his lover La Guiccioli a year earlier, brought it to life. Shelley wrote that it was "a miserable place: the people are barbarous and wild."

The exteriors of Ravenna's churches do little to contradict this opinion. Plain and uninviting, they were built mainly by Christian Romans and their Ostrogoth conquerors in the fifth and sixth centuries. The interiors, however, are filled with resplendent mosaics, in particular San Vitale and the equally gorgeous mausoleum dedicated to Augusta Galla Placidia.

Galla Placidia, the Empress of the West, was the wife, half-sister, and mother of three emperors who ruled from 425 to 440. Her daughter, Honoria, may have begun the Hun invasion with a letter to Attila, in which she enclosed a ring and a plea that he come and rescue her from the convent where her mother had sent her.

Attila jumped at the chance of using marriage to Honoria as a pretext for invading Italy and, in 452, swept into the country. Honoria and Attila never married, and Attila died, so it is said, in the arms of his bride, Illico, in 453.

Basilica di San Vitale
Mausoleo di Galla Placidia
Via Fiandrini

BACKGROUND: *Capital from San Vitale.*

Excursion from Ferrara: Ravenna

*D*ante became the guest of Ravenna's Guido Novello, the Count of Polenta,[1] after his exile from Florence in 1302. When Dante died in 1312, his body was placed in a tomb next to the Church of San Francesco in

A copy of Dante's death mask, given to historian J. A. Symonds.

Tomba di Dante
Chiesa di San Francesco
Via Dante Alighieri 9

" 'Good night, dearest Dante!' well, good
    night!"
—Elizabeth Barrett
Browning, 1851

Ravenna. In 1519, his remains were hidden from Florentines intent on getting him back. But after the Florence delegation left empty-handed, someone forgot to return the bones, and they were lost for the next 350 years.

In 1865, a box of bones suspected to be Dante's turned up in a chapel next to his tomb. They were examined by scientists eager to confirm their identity. First, the skull was favorably compared with the poet's death mask. Then the brain cavity was filled with rice; it held 1,420 grams. (The cranial capacities of Cuvier, Byron, and an insane person measured 1,861 grams, 1,807 grams, and 1,783 grams, respectively.) Finally, the skull's osseous regions were found to be especially developed in the areas of well-being and literature, specifically poetry. Thus, the scientists were satisfied that "the characteristics of a philosophic mind show[ed] themselves" and declared that the bones were indeed Dante's.

1 Polenta is also one of Italy's most famous foods, eaten mostly in central and northern Italy. It was first known as an Etruscan staple made from grains, and was called *puls* or *pulmentum* by the Romans. Today, it consists of cornmeal, cooked either into a cake or into a kind of porridge.

Venezia

Veneziano: native of Venice, dialect of Venice

Veneziana: Venetian blind

Venexiane: Venetian women

"Venice pleases me as much as I expected, and I expected much."—Byron, 1816

"I feel that I've always been in Venice, and that I've never been in Venice at all."
—Paolo Barbaro, *Venice Revealed,* 1998

PREVIOUS PAGE: Travel in Italy, *tourist magazine, c. 1930. Artist uncredited.*
BACKGROUND: *Venice, 1874.*

WHAT IS TO BE MADE of this city that sits on neither land nor water? Is it still an enchantment capable of inspiring a modern-day Byron? Or has it—as bad-tempered Ruskin would say—been chilled by the frosts of the Renaissance and since destroyed by decay and progress? How can the clichés be stopped from tripping over themselves in descriptions of the vistas, the art, the palazzi, the canals? Can you form an independent opinion without being prompted by the whispers of long-gone artists and writers?

Of the many ways to absorb Venice, one of the best is to seek out the guidance of these ghosts—Tintoretto, Byron, James—and have them lead you into their distinct histories. You could try to coax Venice into talking herself, but for a city where sound travels so well, she can be astoundingly mute.

Riding the *gondole, traghetti,* and *vaporetti* (gondolas, ferryboats, and waterbuses) gives views of grand palazzi and outlying islands that would otherwise be missed, but the *calli,* streets, are far more intimate. From deep in the labyrinth comes a silence that speaks volumes. Signposts are layered over signposts; changing street names betray changing fortunes. The streets, if one dares call them that, become ever smaller, squeezing themselves from the

COMVNE DI VENEZIA

Il visitatore è tenuto a conservare il biglietto fino all'uscita. Il biglietto è valido per una sola volta e per il giorno in cui è stato acquistato. Presso il bigliettaio è ostensibile il registro dei reclami. — Nessuna mancia

BIGLIETTO D'INGRESSO

LIRE 12.00

wide *rive* that parallel the Grand Canal, into *fondamente,* then *calli, callette,* and *sottocalli,* until they become so narrow that it seems the only way to pass through them is to be reborn a Venetian. No wonder blinds were named after this city, where there is even a word to describe the rays of light that pass through their narrow slits: *sciabolati,* after *sciaboli,* sabers.

Venice is given its light and life by the watery network that surrounds and permeates it. The reflections create the illusion that this once-grand city still dominates the world, and though, from time to time, you remind yourself that the buildings are little more than facades meant to be viewed by their best angle—much as courtesans skillfully painted their faces to be seen only in a certain setting—still you revel in the deception.

Founded as a refuge and once a mercantile power to be reckoned with, Venice now relies on its past. The very travelers it attracts have contemplated its eternally sinking, crumbling walls and have foretold its demise since the 1700s. The city's stubborn defiance of this prediction may be the key to its survival.

"I had no conception of the excess to which avarice, cowardice, superstition, ignorance, passionless lust, and all the inexpressible brutalities which degrade human nature, could be carried, until I had passed a few days at Venice."—Shelley, 1818

"Venice can only be compared to itself."— Goethe, *Italian Journey,* 1786

BELOW: *Fondaco dei Turchi on the Grand Canal.*

Great Venetian family names include Pisani, Morosini, Vendramin, Foscari, Contarini, Dandolo, Mocenigo, Loredan, Trevisan, and Barbarigo. You'll see them again and again, on doge's tombs and on crumbling palazzi.

The Lion of San Marco, *atop a column in Piazzetta San Marco, keeps St Theodore company.*

VENICE'S ORIGINS

Venice was founded by Romans from Veneto-Friuli who sought shelter in its inaccessible lagoons, after fleeing from the marauding Goths, then Huns. At first the city was only a cluster of temporary settlements. Serious building on reclaimed land began after the Lombard invasion of the eighth century. When Byzantium floundered, Venice declared itself a Republic, spurned the obsolete emperor's choice of patron saint, Theodore (who still stands on a column in the *piazzetta*), and adopted San Marco, Mark the Evangelist, whose body was fetched by Venetians from Alexandria and who is symbolized by lions.

From the ninth century on, Venice grew and prospered. Trading ties with the East were strengthened during the Crusades, through which Venice won exclusive trade concessions. Salt, nutmeg, pepper, opium, and sugar entered Europe through its port.

After successfully battling the Turks and the Genoese to maintain control of the Eastern Mediterranean, Venice's fortunes began to fade in the 16th century, thanks to the Portuguese and their new trade route to India. Napoleon severed its last, lingering hold on power when he became the first invader to conquer it.

VENICE STREETS

Calle: street; *calletta, callesella, sottocalle, microcalle:*
  progressively smaller streets
Campo: square; *campiello, campazzo:* small and
  smaller squares
Corte: courtyard
Fondamenta: street alongside a canal
Liston: promenade, formerly a passageway to
  an ambassador's residence
Passerella: footbridge set up during *acque alte,*
  high waters
Piazza: large square; Venice's only piazza is that
  of San Marco (below).
Piazzetta: small square; Venice has two: San
  Marco and Leone
Piscina: a *campo* that's a filled-in canal
Ponte: bridge; *ponticello:* little bridge
Portico: arcade; *sottoportico:* underpass
Rialto: from *rio alto,* high
  bank alongside a canal
Rio terrà: street that's a
  filled-in canal
Rio: canal; *riotello/riello:*
  little canal
Riva: wide *fondamenta*
Ruga: street lined with shops,
  from the French *rue*
Struscio: weekend
  promenade, from
  strusciare, to rub together

Venetian street names
such as Riva degli
Incurabili, Street of
the Incurables, and
Calle Pensieri, Street
of Thoughts, are
descriptive. But few
match Ponte e
Fondamenta della
Tette, Bridge and
Street of the Tits,
between Campi San
Cassiano and San
Polo, named for
16th-century prosti-
tutes who leaned out
the windows, baring
their breasts.

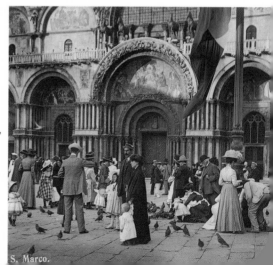

S. Marco.

Doges sported an odd rimless hat known as a *corno*. It was encircled by a gold brocade band and had a bump rising out of the top rear portion. It sat over the *vittà*, a white cotton cap from which hung ear flaps and dangling strings. The doge's robe was called the *dogalina*.

Museo Storico Navale
Campo San Biagio,
Arsenale

THE DOGE

A Venetian doge (meaning, roughly, duke) was elected for life, a life that was often very brief, especially for those who overstepped their authority. Many were assassinated, executed, blinded, or exiled. Doges presided over the Signoria, a cabinet of three judges and six representatives from the city's six *sestieri,* sections. The first certain doge was Orso Ipato, who held the post from 726 to 737.

As a figurehead, the doge took part in ceremonies such as his "marriage" to the Adriatic. This peculiar tradition involved throwing a ring into the sea and proclaiming domination over its waters. It was first held in the year 1000 to commemorate a Venetian victory over Slav pirates. In 1177, it became an annual event, thereafter celebrating the defeat of Emperor Frederick I.

On Ascension Day, the doge boarded the state galley, the cumbrous, ornate *Il Bucintoro* (left), and was rowed out. He flung his ring into the Adriatic, then returned. Spectators must have held their collective breaths, wondering if this was the day the ship would sink and allow the union to finally take place.

In 1797, Napoleon persuaded the last of 120 doges, Ludovico Manin, to step down, then stripped the *Bucintoro* of its gold. A replica is found in the Museo Storico Navale.

DOGES OF DISTINCTION

Marino Faliero's term began inauspiciously, when his official arrival was delayed by fog. As he made his way through the *piazzetta,* he walked between the columns where criminals were executed. Seven months later, under the charge of treasonously grasping for supreme power, he was beheaded.

What grander place for this to take place than the top of the Scala dei Giganti, Giants' Staircase (page 61), of the gothic Palazzo Ducale? That's where Byron and Casimir Delavigne each placed Faliero's beheading in their respective epic versions of the event. But his head did not roll down those stairs—they were built more than a hundred years later.

Faliero's portrait in the Sala di Maggior Consiglio is shown as a painted black cloth, inscribed "Hic est locus Marini Faledri decapitati pro criminibus" (This is the place of Marino Faliero, who was decapitated for his crime).

The longest-reigning doge appears to have been Francesco Foscari. For 34 years, from 1423 to 1457, Foscari oversaw Venice's affairs and put his name to numerous villas, one of which was Ca' Foscari, now the Biblioteca Generale di Venezia. Foscari had been forced by the Council of Ten—formed to hand down sentences against those who committed crimes

Faliero was caught in a *nebbia,* fog. But was it a *nebbietta* or *nebbiolino,* mist; *nebbia spessa* or *nebbiaccia,* dense fog; *nebbiaio,* foggy weather; or *nebbione,* thick fog? Other foggy Venetian words include *nebbiosità,* fogginess; *nebulosità,* mistiness; and *nebuloso,* foggy.

Sala di Maggior Consiglio
Palazzo Ducale
Piazzetta San Marco

Ca' Foscari
Biblioteca Generale di Venezia
Canal Grande
Vaporetto Ca' Rezzonico

BACKGROUND: *Capital from the Palazzo Ducale (15th century).*

Some families supplied many doges even though the position was not supposed to be hereditary:

Participazios: Seven doges between 811 and 942

Contarini: Eight doges between 1043 and 1684

Mocenigos: Seven doges between 1414 and 1778

Chiesa Santa Maria Gloriosa dei Frari

Campo dei Frari

against the state—to banish his own son, Jacopo, on three different occasions. Although eventually found innocent of the charges against him, Jacopo died in prison. Foscari wept when he heard of his son's death, and for doing so he was accused of imbecility. Steps were taken to depose him. He died of a broken blood vessel caused by the sound of the bell announcing the succession of Pasquale Malipiero. His tomb is at Santa Maria Gloriosa dei Frari.

The Council of Ten had their ears and eyes on everyone and everything. No one was free of their scrutiny, least of all the doge. Even pillow talk was risky, as a listening post apparently had been set up to catch bedtime gossip between doge and dogaressa.[1]

 Also interred at the Frari, Giovanni Pesaro, doge for only one year, 1658–59, died when he fell down a secret staircase in the Palazzo. Of his tomb by Baldassare Longhena, *Cook's* wrote, "the ponderous mausoleum presses with crushing weight on the shoulders of four unhappy negroes [*sic*], black as the blackest marble can make them; their sable knees bursting through their white drawers in their desperate efforts to sustain their burden."

1 The dogaressa was ornamental and had minimal duties, aside from appearing with her husband at functions.

A Famous Venetian
GIOVANNI GIACOMO CASANOVA: 1725–98

The otherwise splendid Doge's Palace has two quarters of ill repute: the *pozzi* (lower dungeons) and the *piombi* (lead chambers under the roof),[2] still haunted by ghosts of prisoners past, such as disreputable Casanova,

Palazzo Ducale
Piazza San Marco

"I feel remorse for nothing and I am therefore guilty of nothing."—Casanova, 1756

Venetian adventurer, rake, librarian, and one-time candidate for priesthood.

Before his incarceration, Casanova had traveled extensively. After returning to Venice—he lived at the Palazzo Malipiero, near Campo San Samuele—he was arrested for cabalism (black magic), freemasonry (corruption of Christians), literary criticism, scandalous behavior, or simply consorting with the wrong side. He was sentenced to five years in the *piombi* and, after spending 1755 and 1756 there, escaped with great aplomb and derring-do, aided by Father Balbi, a fellow prisoner.

Casanova then dallied around Europe, fought duels, rented palatial mansions, bilked rich women, wrote plays, and fortified his reputation as a libertine. He returned to Venice as a hired spy but was exiled when he verbally attacked the ruling family. He died in 1798, after writing 12 volumes of memoirs and becoming a librarian for Count Walstein, at Duchcov in Bohemia, now the Czech Republic. He was buried in Duchcov, but his remains were removed and have since been lost.

2 Join the *Itinerari Segreti*, Secret Itinerary tours, offered, in Italian only, by the Palazzo Ducale.

Venetian Relics Itinerary

SAN MARCO: Basilica di San Marco, *Piazza San Marco*

The body of Venice's patron saint, St Mark, was shipped to Venice from Alexandria around A.D. 800, hidden under a load of pork to discourage Muslim customs agents from snooping. His remains then disappeared in 976 during a fire in the Basilica but miraculously reappeared in 1094 upon consecration of the new building.

SANTA LUCIA: Chiesa di San Geremia, *Campo San Geremia*

St Lucy, patron saint of Syracuse, was brought to the Church of Santa Lucia after being stolen from Constantinople. When the church was torn down to make way for the train station, the saint was moved to nearby San Geremia. She is so popular in Scandinavia, it's surprising that Swedes have not attempted to abduct her.

MARC ANTONIO BRAGADIN: Santi Giovanni e Paolo (San Zanipolo)
Campo Santi Giovanni e Paolo

In 1571, just before the Battle of Lepanto between Turkey and Venice, Bragadin, Venetian governor to Cyprus, was negotiating with the Turks in Famagosta, when he ended up being "flayed alive," but not before facing the executioner three times, having his nose (some say ears, others say both) cut off and suffering other indignities. His skin was stuffed with hay and taken to Constantinople, where it was paraded through the city streets. His family bought it back and laid it to rest in Santi Giovanni e Paolo, where you can also find Santa Caterina di Siena's foot. The rest of her is at Santa Maria sopra Minerva in Rome, except for her thumb and head, which are in Siena.

SANCTA CATHARINA DESENIS.

A Famous Visitor
HESTER PIOZZI: 1741–1821

Hester Piozzi traveled through Italy from 1784 to 1786 with her second husband, Gabriele Piozzi. Whereas she was fleeing English society and its disapproval of her marriage to an insignificant foreigner, her husband was evading her creditors, for she had contracted significant debts. Piozzi, who stayed in Venice in 1785, had this to say about Venetians and their coffee:

Hester Piozzi would have taken her coffee at one of these still-existing *caffè* on the Piazza San Marco:

Florian's
Est. 1720 by Floriano Francesconi. This *caffè* was a base for patriots during the 1840s.

Caffè Quadri
Est. 1775 by Giorgio Quadri. Austrian soldiers met here to watch patriots watching them from Florian's.

Gran Caffè Lavena
Est. 18th century. Composer Richard Wagner was a frequent customer.

Venice's vicinity to Turkey has . . . made them contract some similarity of manners; for what, except being imbued with Turkish notions, can account for the people's rage here, young and old, rich and poor, to pour down such quantities of coffee? I have already had seven cups to-day, and feel frightened lest we should some of us be killed with so strange an abuse of it. On the opposite shore, across the Adriatic, opium[3] is taken to counteract its effects; but these dear Venetians have no notion of sleep being necessary to their existence . . . as some or other of them seem constantly in motion, and there is really no hour of the four-and-twenty in which the town seems perfectly still and quiet.—*Glimpses of Italian Society,* 1892

3 Opium was a key ingredient in the Venetian panacea known as theriac.

A Famous Visitor
JOHN RUSKIN: 1819–1900

English art critic John Ruskin, a denouncer of excess and a champion
of Gothic purity, wrote prolifically on Italian art and architecture.
Venice, especially, fascinated him, though he found much to criticize:

No one has ever believed a word I said, though the public have from the
first done me the honour to praise my manner of saying it; and, as far as
they found the things I spoke of amusing to themselves, they have deigned
for a couple of days or so to look at them, helped always through the
tedium of the business by due quantity of ices at Florian's, music by
moonlight on the Grand Canal, paper-lamps, and the English papers and
magazines at M. Ongaria's, with such illumination as those New Lamps
contain—Lunar or Gaseous, enabling pursy Britannia to compare, at her
ease, her own culminating and co-operate Prosperity and Virtue with the
past wickedness and present out-of-pocketness of the umquhile Queen of
the Sea.

Allowing to the full for the extreme unpleasantness of the facts recorded
in this book to the mind of a people set wholly on the pursuit of the same
pleasures which ruined Venice; only in ways as
witless as hers were witty; I think I can now see
a further reason for their non-acceptance of the
book's teaching, namely, the entire concealment of
my own personal feelings throughout, which gives
a continual look of insincerity to my best passages.
—*The Stones of Venice,* 1881

Ruskin favored such
Venetian buildings as
the Basilica di San
Marco and the
Palazzo Ducale. He
was also ecstatic over
Tintoretto's paintings
in the Scuola di San
Rocco.

BACKGROUND: *Ruskin's own illustration of Venetian arches.*

Napoleon the Looter
NAPOLEON BONAPARTE: 1769–1821

$\mathcal{I}$n 1796, Napoleon, as commander-in-chief of the French army in Italy, aimed to drain the country of every piece of valuable art he could lay his hands on. His success was apparent, as long caravans of booty (some paid for, most not) rolled into Paris. Notable works of art, such as the *Laocoön*, Titian's *Christ,* and Raphael's *Transfiguration* (all from Rome), were destined to enrich Paris's magnificent Louvre. Others, such as the horses of Piazza San Marco, were to grace public spaces. Venice also lost jewels from the Pala d'Oro in the Basilica di San Marco and the winged lion from atop the column in the Piazzetta di San Marco, a heartily symbolic theft, as the lion, which represents Venice's patron saint, San Marco, *is* Venice. Also taken were bibelots from various palazzi and numerous Tintorettos, Veroneses, and other paintings and statues.

Napoleon's mania extended to artists, as he tried to lure the likes of Antonio Canova to Paris with promises of untold wealth. Canova visited Paris but refused to move there and, after Napoleon's abdication, was directed to arrange for the return of the works to Italy. Around 1,000 paintings, 300 sculptures, and as many as 20,000 drawings were stolen from all of Italy.

It's difficult to imagine how Napoleon transported the Horses of San Marco, also known as

Antonio Canova

1757–1822

Canova studied in Venice but lived mostly in Rome. He sculpted nudes of Napoleon and of Napoleon's sister Pauline. His bronze Napoleon in Roman armor is at the Pinocateca di Brera, Milan.

Canova's right hand is at the Gallerie dell'Accademia, his heart is at the Santa Maria Gloriosa dei Frari, and the rest of him is in his home town, Possagno, near Vicenzo.

the *Quadriga,* to Paris. These four bronze horses, displayed on the top terrace of the Basilica di San Marco, weigh about two tons apiece and had been brought to Venice as booty from Constantinople in 1204.[4] Napoleon took them to Paris, via the Alps, through his newly constructed Simplon Pass, and had them placed on the Triumphal Arch[5] in the Place du Carrousel. They were returned to Venice in 1815, were sent briefly to Rome for safety during WWI, then subsequently were moved to the Museo di San Marco. Copies now stand in their place.

La discesa dei cavalli, *The Descent of the Horses, San Marco, Venice, c. 1916.*

Napoleon also stole Pope Pius VII (left), sending him to Fontainebleau. The pope refused to recognize Napoleon as king of Italy, then excommunicated him when Napoleon declared the Papal States nonexistent.

"I shall be an Attila to the State of Venice."
—Napoleon

4 The horses are thought to date from the fourth or third century B.C. They were made by Lysippus of Chios, Greece, or are of Roman origin.

5 The Triumphal Arch had been built to look like Rome's Arch of Severus, one of the few pieces of Italy that Napoleon couldn't figure out how to cart to Paris.

Venetian Condotierri

Venice was the headquarters of two especially powerful *condotierri,* mercenaries: Francesco Bussone, best known as Carmagnola, and Bartolomeo Colleoni.

A protégé of the mighty Milanese *condotierre* Facio Cane, Carmagnola, from Piedmont, became one of Italy's greatest mercenary soldiers at the age of 22, when Cane's untimely death pushed him into Milan's circle of power. From then on, he walked a tightrope between the rival powers of Milan and Venice. His end came in 1432 while he was working for the Venetians. Accused of conspiring with Filippo-Maria Visconti of Milan, he was lured to Venice—away from the protection of his loyal army— and was tortured in the dungeon of the Doge's Palace, then beheaded on Piazzetta San Marco.

Bartolomeo Colleoni, from Bergamo in Lombardy, joined up with a Neapolitan *condotierre* at an early age. He then moved to Carmagnola's Venetian forces in 1429. After Carmagnola's death, Colleoni rose rapidly to the position of commander. His fortunes grew as Venice rewarded him liberally for his services. But when Venice cut back its mercenary budget in 1443, he defected to Filippo-Maria Visconti of Milan. He returned to Venice but defected again, once more considering himself undervalued. By the time he died in 1475, he had made his peace with Venice.

His statue by Andrea Verrocchio shows fierce, piercing eyes and a skeletal face. Colleoni would be disappointed with the statue's location, however; he had bequeathed his wealth to Venice to guarantee that the statue would be prominently placed in Piazza San Marco. Instead, the city fathers, who had no intention of ceding such an important position to a *condotierre,* tucked it away in Campo Santi Giovanni e Paolo.

FACING PAGE AND BACKGROUND: *The statue of Bartolomeo Colleoni.*

Palazzo del Cammello
Campo dei Mori

Casa di Tintoretto
*Fondamenta dei
Mori 3399*

Scuola Grande di San Rocco
Campo San Rocco

LEVANTINE VENICE

The Cannaregio district northeast of the Santa
Lucia station has Venice's Ghetto, or Jewish quarter, a feverish daily market, and a few cheapish
hotels, but for visitors searching out remnants of
the city's connection with the East, the Square
of the Moors and Jacopo Robusti Tintoretto's
house just off the square are the most com-
pelling reasons to explore the neighborhood.

Three turbaned Moors guard the square and
give it its name. Although these Moors may
have actually been silk merchants from Morea,
in the Peloponnese, the oriental imagery is
compounded by a stone camel relief (left)
embedded into a wall of their former house,
the Palazzo del Cammello. It is found on the
east side of the square.

A turbaned Moor stands before the house
Tintoretto lived in for 20 years until his death in
1594. Tintoretto, literally "little dyer," after his
father's profession, was also nicknamed *furioso,* for
the energy he put into his painting. On the
subject of speed, it has been said that he "finished a painting before anyone even knew he
had started." It is estimated that he painted more
than 700 works; finding all of them might take
longer than it took him to paint them. A
good place to start is the Scuola Grande di San
Rocco, which has some 50 of his biblical scenes.

Palazzi on the Grand Canal Itinerary

Most of Venice's grand private homes, the palazzi, date from the 15th century or later and have had plenty of time to accumulate thick layers of lore. Some, like the Dandolo and the Gritti, were built for doges; others, like the Labia, were for wealthy merchants. Many are now hotels. A number have similar and confusing names, as they were lived in by a succession of families. To make matters worse, some are known alternatively as *Ca',* house, a less grand term for the same thing.

Each palazzo has an *androne,* ground floor, consisting of storage, an entrance, possibly a boathouse, and perhaps a courtyard; a *mezzanino,* where business was conducted; and a *piano nobile,* noble floor, for receiving guests. The upper floors are living and servant's quarters.

GIUSTINIAN and PALAZZI LOREDAN-VENDRAMIN-CALERGI:
Vaporetti San Marcuola or Ca' Rezzonico

On a visit in 1858–59, German composer Richard Wagner stayed in the Palazzo Giustinian, where he composed the second act of *Tristan und Isolde* on his own piano, after having had it and his bed shipped to Venice. More than 20 years later, suffering from overwork and ill health, he returned to Venice and this time took up residence at the Palazzo Loredan-Vendramin-Calergi (right, now the Winter Casino). He died here in February 1883. The plaque commemorating his stay was written by Gabriele D'Annunzio, who wrote eulogistically of Wagner's death in his novel *Il fuoco, The Flame* (1900).

PALAZZO MANGILLI-VALMARANA: *Vaporetto Rio dei Santi Apostoli*

Now the Argentinean Consulate, in the 18th century this palazzo was home to British consul Joseph Smith, also known as the Merchant of Venice, because of all his complex negotiations in the art world. A patron of artists such as Antonio Canaletto and Rosalba Carriera, he wiped out the fortune of his rich, unstable, opera-singer wife, spending much of it on his abundant and well-chosen collection of art and books, which he eventually sold to England's King George III. Smith was buried in the Catholic Cemetery on the Lido but was later moved to St George Anglican Church, Dorsoduro.

PALAZZO MOCENIGO: *Vaporetti San Samuele or Sant'Angelo*

The four buildings that make up this complex were built by the Mocenigo family, suppliers of seven of Venice's doges. Today, it is best remembered as the 1818–19 residence of Byron; his illegitimate daughter, Allegra; and his menagerie of odd pets and mistresses.

PALAZZO BENZON: *Vaporetto Sant'Angelo*

Byron lived within swimming distance of the Palazzo Benzon, so he would often dive into the Grand Canal and take the watery route home after attending, along with Canova, Stendhal, and other artists and writers, the evening *conversazioni,* receptions, of Contessa Maria Benzon. Benzon was known for having donned a Greek tunic to dance the Carmagnole[6] in Piazza San Marco when the French entered Venice. When out and about, Benzon, like her Venetian sisters, would tuck a piece of polenta between her breasts to keep it warm for when she got hungry.

6 The Carmagnole, after the Piedmont town of the same name, was a dance created to celebrate the French Revolution.

PALAZZO PISANI MORETTA:
Vaporetto Rio di San Polo

Palazzo Pisani Moretta was owned by Nicolo Pisani, a member of the Great Council, in the early 1300s. Paolo Veronese is reputed to have left a painting rolled up under one of the beds as a token of his gratitude for hospitality shown him.

PALAZZO VENIER DEI LEONI: *Vaporetto Salute*

Nowadays, people visit the one-story Palazzo Venier dei Leoni (also called "Nonfinito" because of its unfinished state) for its collection of art assembled by Peggy Guggenheim, a wealthy and eccentric American. She was buried at her palazzo in 1979, along with her 14 dogs. A more infamous resident was Luisa Casati, the fashionable and cadaverously thin daughter of a Milanese industrialist, who voraciously consumed an immense fortune thanks to her extravagant lifestyle. She married the Marchese Casati, then was seduced by novelist Gabriele D'Annunzio. She adopted white pancake makeup and heavy black eyeliner, dyed her hair flame red, wore outfits that self-destructed in rain or wind for shock value, and paraded about Europe's capitals with an odd assortment of pets, including snakes. While living in Venice from about 1910 to 1924, Casati would stroll nude at night through Piazza San Marco with her pet cheetahs, a black escort lighting her way. Her fortune ravaged, she moved to London and occupied a squalid bed-sit until her death in 1957.

CASINA ROSSA: *Vaporetto Santa Maria del Giglio*

Gabriele D'Annunzio, novelist, playwright, poet, soldier, and statesman, lived at this former studio of Canova's during WWI. On an earlier stay in the city, he had begun an affair with actress Eleanora Duse; their first romantic encounter took place at the Hotel Danieli.

D'Annunzio, already notorious for his impassioned novels, shocked the world during WWII when he claimed Fiume (now Rijeka, Croatia) for Italy, creating an illegal government there. He died in 1938.

HOTEL DANIELI: *Riva degli Schiavoni 4196*

In 1834, writer George Sand left her husband and traveled with Alfred de Musset (below) from Paris to Venice. Their first days at the luxurious Danieli were spent struggling with bouts of diarrhea. Musset was mortified that friends might get wind of their humiliating affliction, but he improved quickly, went carousing, and picked up gonorrhea. He then developed bronchitis and briefly went mad. Neglected, Sand fell for his physician, Dr Pagallo. Thus spurned, Musset flounced back to France alone. Sand's *Lettres d'un voyageur* recounts the year she spent with Pagallo.

Originally built for Doge Dandolo in the early 1300s, the palazzo became the Albergo Reale in 1822. Guests have included Balzac, Ruskin, Dickens, Wagner, Debussy, Cocteau, and Proust. It's here D'Annunzio and Duse began their affair.

Henry James, author of *The Aspen Papers* and *The Wings of the Dove,* visited Venice many years later and found that Sand's story still captivated the "Sandists." "Why," he asked, "are we fond observer[s] of the footprints of genius?" Little did he realize that "Jamesists" would make similar pilgrimages to his Venetian homes, the Palazzo Barbaro and Pensione Wildner.

Excursion from Venice: Villa Pisani

Villa Pisani at Strà, southwest of Venice, was built by Doge Alvise Pisani in the 1730s. A former diplomat, Alvise was immensely wealthy and commissioned Tiepolo to paint a superb fresco, *The Apotheosis of the Pisani Family,* in the grand central hall.

Napoleon bought the villa in 1807, then gave it to his stepson, Eugène de Beauharnais, the Prince of Venice, after sleeping in the custom-made gold and lacquer bed only once. In 1817, exiled Spanish King Carlos IV, his wife, Maria Louisa of Parma, and her lover, Manuel de Godoy, stayed here for two months. Hitler and Mussolini met at the villa in 1934.

Girolamo Frigimelica of Padua designed many of the villa's features, including a box-wood labyrinth. At the maze's center is a tower with an exterior winding staircase. An observer standing atop the tower can shout out directions to souls lost in the labyrinth's confusing depths, which is precisely how D'Annunzio's hero Stelio rescued his heroine in *The Flame.* In this enchanting novel, the narrator's mistress (D'Annunzio's real-life mistress, actress Eleanora Duse) briefly loses herself and her reason in the maze's paths. Echoing voices—sometimes very close and other times inconceivably far away— add to her confusion and distress. Finally, the caretaker climbs the tower and guides her out.

"Neglect and age had turned [the labyrinth] wild and desolate, had removed every trace of lightheartedness and regularity, transforming it into an enclosed brownish-yellow patch of undergrowth, full of inextricable circumlocutions, where the slanting rays of the setting sun so reddened bushes that they were like bonfires that burned without smoke."—Gabriele D'Annunzio, *The Flame,* 1900

Excursions from Venice: Palladian Villas
ANDREA PALLADIO: 1508–80

*A*rchitect and author of *I quattro libri dell'architettura*, Palladio has become synonymous with the word *temple* because of his classically proportioned buildings found mostly at Vicenza, but also in Venice and surroundings. His often-imitated Villa Rotonda, near Vicenza, is characterized by its four stately and identical sides.

Villa Rotonda, the setting for Joseph Losey's film Don Giovanni.

Villa Foscari (Malcontenta), near Fusina.

Palladio also designed the Villa Foscari, aka Malcontenta, accessible by boat along the Brenta Canal. Built for two Foscari brothers in the late 1550s, this large villa has a gorgeous series of frescoes by Veronese and Giambattista Zelotti. Because of its name, people look for unhappiness, but its discontent is elusive. Was it named for an inconstant *contessa* who was abandoned here to mope in solitude? Or does it come from the villa's somewhat isolated and lonely appearance? No one seems to know, but the area was apparently known as Malcontenta before the Foscaris arrived.

Back in Venice, Palladio designed the Redentore, on Giudecca, a tribute to the end of the plague. But Palladio, with his devotion to all sides of a building, didn't fare as well in Venice, where facades tend to rule supreme, as he did in the countryside, where his skill could be admired.

Padova

Padova

DURING ITS ROMAN YEARS as *Patavium,* Padua was second only to Rome in wealth, but the Huns reduced it to a shambles in 452. It was eclipsed by Venice in the 9th and 10th centuries, and what glory it could regain came from the university, established in the early 1200s. Since the early 19th century, a *caffè* is the attraction that has drawn visitors.

Caffè Pedrocchi, founded by Antonio Pedrocchi, was in operation 24 hours a day, seven days a week when it first opened. It became a center for Risorgimento meetings in 1848, and in 1885 the *Guide diamant* called it Italy's most remarkable *caffè,* because the owner wouldn't permit smoking. *Baedeker's,* enamored with its glorious décor, named it "the pride of the town." U. S. consul W. D. Howells observed it to be "a granite edifice of Egyptian architecture, which is the mausoleum of the proprietor's fortune." Pedrocchi's was given to the city in 1891. After a brief closure for renovations, the bar and restaurant are again functioning, and the upstairs rooms, featuring architectural themes—Etruscan, Roman, Renaissance, Greek, Gothic, and Egyptian—are open to the public.

Before Pedrocchi's opened, Stendhal recommended the Caffè del principe Carlo, "where all the good-looking women go."

Caffè Pedrocchi
Via VIII Febbraio 15
Piazzetta Pedrocchi

Giovanni and Sarah Belzoni
Padua has Egyptian artifacts, thanks to Giovanni Belzoni, explorer, archaeologist, and six-foot-six circus strongman, and his wife, Sarah, an English giantess. In 1816, the couple went to Egypt hoping that Giovanni could get work as a hydraulic engineer; he ended up excavating Abu Simbel.

PREVIOUS PAGE: *The house of the poet Petrarch at Arquà Petrarca, near Padua.*

ANATOMY IN PADUA

You can probably name explorers who have had geographical features named after them, or botanists whose names are attached to specific plants. But what about parts of the body named after anatomists? Of the Paduan anatomists, Gabrielo Fallopio (1523–62), a syphilitic mercenary turned anatomy professor and sometime priest, left his name in the female reproductive parts. Andreas Vesalius (1514–64), the Flemish author of *De humani corporis fabrica, The Fabric of the Human Body,* and Padua's most famous anatomy lecturer, had only minor features, such as the small holes in the base of the skull known as the "foramen of Vesalius," named after him.

Another eponymously linked anatomist was Bartolomeo Eustachio (1520–74). He understood how the eyes are raised and lowered, making him the anatomist of the wink and the blink. But his real claim to fame is the eustachian tube, the canal that connects the ear to the throat.

The anatomy theater in the Palazzo del Bo, so called after a tavern on the site that sported the sign of an ox, dates from around 1594. The courtyard and hallways are open during teaching hours, and travelers with the special goal of following Galileo's tracks will be interested to know that he taught physics here from 1592 until 1610.

Teatro Anatomico
Palazzo del Bo
Via VIII Febbraio 2
(hours very irregular)

Many professors who couldn't have body parts named after them bequeathed their own to the university. Their skulls can be seen at the Anatomy Department, also located in the Palazzo del Bo.

BACKGROUND: *Illustration of brains and nerves from Eustachio's* Tabulæ Anatomicæ, *1714.*

Cappella degli Scrovegni
Giardini dell'Arena
Piazza Eremitani
(advance booking
necessary)

Infidelity, *one of the allegorical figures in the series
of Virtues and Vices,
Cappella degli Scrovegni.*

A GLORIOUS REDEMPTION

Rinaldo degli Scrovegni, a Paduan known as
"moneybags," was so unscrupulously usurious
that he was denied a Christian burial. His son
Enrico, in atonement for his father's sins, built
this compact chapel, also known as the Church
of the Madonna dell'Arena, and commissioned
a series of frescoes from Giotto, carried out
between 1303 and 1305.

This pious act did not keep the elder
Scrovegni out of Dante's *Inferno* (Canto 17),
however. He was placed into Circle Seven, the
Hell of Violence. In the usurer's instance, this
referred to violence against nature. Sinners
such as Scrovegni became shades seated on red-
hot sand, doomed to look perpetually upon the
ground. Scrovegni's usurious companions were
Vialiano dei Vitaliani, another Paduan, as well
as several Florentines. Dante's Scrovegni complained that the Florentines continually shouted
in his ear.

Arranged in a series of three bands, the
frescoes are miracles of coloring, naturalism, and
use of space. They depict the story of Christian
redemption and include the Expulsion of
Joachim from the Temple, the Last Judgment,
and a group of allegorical Virtues and Vices.

An Eccentric Visitor
EDWARD WORTLEY MONTAGU: 1713–76

Edward, the no-good son of the extraordinary traveler Lady Mary Wortley Montagu, lived in both Venice and Padua but died in Padua, it's said of an infected throat after choking on a bone from a small bird.

Lady Mary, a woman of the world, epistolarian, and energetic commentator on life, was a phenomenon. Edward was a phenomenal lunatic: gambler, rake, dilettante, linguist, liar, revolutionary, and possibly author, though his claim to have written *Reflections on the Rise and Fall of the Ancient Republicks* was disputed by a contemporary.

He was distinguished at an early age as the first Briton to be inoculated against smallpox. Lady Mary had brought the practice to England after her stay in Constantinople in 1717–18.

A perpetual wanderer, Edward traveled to the West Indies and the Middle East and throughout Europe. He talked his second wife into marriage by convincing her that her still-living husband was dead, then briefly abandoned her in Lebanon. He later left her for a woman described as "Nubian."

In 1742, Lady Mary, who despaired over him, wrote that he was so weak-minded as to be capable of being a monk one day and a Turk three days later. She left him a guinea when she died in 1762.

Edward often dressed in extravagant Turkish clothing.

Excursion from Padua: Arquà Petrarca

PETRARCH: 1304–74

Casa di Petrarca

Arquà Petrarca,
Euganean Hills,
24 km / 15 mi. south-
west of Padua

𝒫oet Francesco Petrarca, known as Petrarch, was educated in the south of France and lived in both Provence and Italy. His frequent bouts of melancholy were intensified by his thwarted love for a woman named Laura, who was married to someone else and didn't give a fig for him. He expressed his love in sonnets, for which he was crowned poet laureate in Rome, in 1341. His works include *De vita solitaria, On Solitary Life; Rime, Rhymes;* and *Trionfi, Triumphs.*

Although he declared his love for Laura to be pure, he is credited with praying "Lord give me chastity, but not just yet," and he had two illegitimate children with an unknown mother.

Petrarch loathed Dante, even though his status as a poet was assured. Among his patrons were the wealthy and powerful Colonna family of Rome. In 1362, he was given a house on the Grand Canal by the Venetian Republic. He lived his last three years at Arquà Petrarca.

His house and tomb can be visited.[1] If you go, you'll be joining a long line of admirers, Petrarchisti. Mozart and Byron, among others, signed the guest book and saw his embalmed, stuffed cat. W. D. Howells noted in 1864 that it had lost its fur.

---

1 Scientists unearthed Petrarch's remains in 2004 in hopes of reconstructing his features. They knew his skull had been dug up, studied, and damaged in the 19th century, but they were certain that modern technology would surmount any difficulties. What they didn't expect, however, was to find that the poet's skull had been replaced by a woman's.

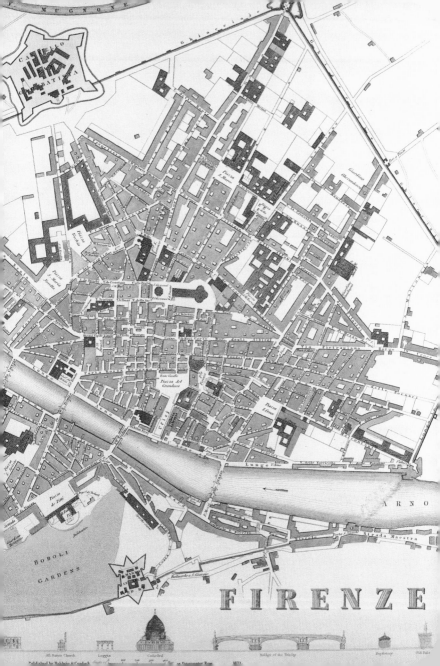

FIRENZE

Published by Baldwin & Cradock, Paternoster Row. 1835.

All Saints Church.   Loggia.   Cathedral.   Bridge of the Trinity.   Baptistery.   Old Palace.

Firenze

"Magnificently stern and sombre are the streets of beautiful Florence; and the strong old piles of building make such heaps of shadow, on the ground and in the river, that there is another and a different city of rich forms and fancies, always lying at our feet."
—Charles Dickens, 1844

"No one believed in the natural death of a prince: Princes must be poisoned or poignarded."
—J. A. Symonds, 1888

PREVIOUS PAGE: *Florence, c. 1835.*
BACKGROUND: *Michelangelo's cartoon,* Soldiers Bathing in the Arno, *detail, c. 1503.*

DANTE CALLED FLORENCE *la bellissima e famosissima figlia di Roma,* the most beautiful and most famous daughter of Rome. Despite this accolade, it's also considered Italy's most austere, most masculine city. Today, as far as superlatives go, it's one of the noisiest, thanks to heavy traffic.

Florence has a history of gruesome murders. In 1342, henchmen for the loathsome tyrant Gualtiero di Brienne were thrown to the crowd in the Piazza della Signoria, hacked into bits, and eaten. Di Brienne was expelled the following year. A hundred years later, Republican soldier Baldaccio de'Anghiari was lured into the Palazzo Vecchio (facing page), run through with swords, decapitated, and left exposed on the piazza.

Florence's most powerful families, the Medici, Strozzi, and Pazzi, continually fought for control of the city. As a result, assassination was an all too common cause of death. W. D. Howells commented that Florentines "tempt the observer to a certain mood of triviality, by their indefatigable antics in cutting and thrusting, chopping off heads, mutilating, burning, and banishing."

With the violence in Florence's history, is it any wonder that its patron saint is John the Baptist, often depicted with his head on a plate? The city, which seems never to have had

Firenze
Cortile di Palazzo Vecchio

a coat of arms, could have adopted the scaffold, sword, and flame as its symbols.

It's time to cease speaking of miserable deaths (except for Savonarola's, which is unavoidable), otherwise we'd talk of nothing else. But wait, there's one more thing: the Arno, Dante's "accursed and unlucky ditch," which was forced to swallow countless suicides, murder victims, and executed felons. It may seem acquiescent, at times insignificant, but it can be vicious; in 1966, it overflowed its banks and spewed centuries-old mud everywhere, from the adjacent houses to the Biblioteca Nazionale. Revenge, you might think, for the atrocities it has been forced to accept.

The best way for those with overactive imaginations to relish Florence's nasty past is to venture out in the dark, after the crowds have disappeared. Distant footsteps, echoing down the narrow, cobblestoned lanes, send shivers down the spine; dim streetlights transform the shadows of harmless passersby into ominous threats; the late-night peal of bells from campaniles provokes grim thoughts of hasty burials.

Nighttime is also when the fashion spies come out. If you're lucky, you'll see them on chic Via Tornabuoni, snapping clandestine pics of shop windows.

"The Arno would be a plausible river if they would pump some water into it. They all call it river, and they honestly think it *is* a river." —Mark Twain, a connoisseur of real rivers like the Mississippi, scoffing at the Arno, *Innocents Abroad,* 1869

"At seven o'clock in the evening, throughout the city, there is a prolonged rumble that sounds as if it were thunder; the blinds are being rolled up to let in the exhausted day."—Mary McCarthy, *The Stones of Florence,* 1959

Casa di Dante

*Via Santa Margherita 1,
corner of Via Dante
Alighieri*

Dante probably did
not live in this house,
now a small museum
honoring him. Some
claim the building
was a wine shop,
frequented by
Michelangelo and
Cellini.

Sasso di Dante

Piazza del Duomo 17

Danteggiare: to imitate
Dante's style

When exiled, Dante
wandered widely.
Strangers would
remark: "Behold, there
is a man who has
been in hell."

BACKGROUND: *One of
many visual interpretations
of Dante's Purgatory,
c. 1860.*

DANTE ALIGHIERI

Although Dante's political affilia-
tions caused him to be expelled
from Florence in 1302, he posthumously became her darling when city officials
realized that there was profit to be made from
his growing fame. Best known for the *Inferno,
Purgatorio,* and *Paradiso*—the *Divina commedia,
Divine Comedy*[1]—he was also the author of
numerous other books, including the *Vita nuova,*
translated as *New* or *Young Life,* about his passion
for Beatrice Portinari, who also became his
literary companion in *Paradiso.*

Dante was probably born on Via San
Martino, now Via Dante Alighieri. If you are
tracking him through Florence, you should
go to the south side of the Piazza del Duomo.
There you'll find the Sasso di Dante, Dante's
Stone, a plain slab upon which he used to sit
and gaze at the church. You can't sit on it, as it's
now part of the wall, but while contemplating
it, you can plan your trip to Ravenna to see
where Dante's bones are kept.

It was Dante's commitment as a White
Guelf in Florence's drawn-out and destructive
dispute between the Whites and the Blacks that
got him tossed out of the city.

The Guelfs and their archenemies, the

1 Dante called it a comedy, because it began darkly and
ended on a light note.

German composer Franz Liszt wrote *Après une lecture du Dante: Fantasia quasi sonato,* inspired by reading Dante.

Chiesa di San Martino
Piazza San Martino
In 1291, Dante married Gemma Donati in this church. After he was exiled, they never saw each other again. At least two of his seven children wrote commentaries on his *Commedia.*

Ghibellines, were two groups competing for power in many Italian cities. Their names came from rival German families, who disputed the throne of the Holy Roman emperor, which had been established in the 12th century and challenged the power of the pope. The Guelfs supported the pope and opposed the German emperors; the Ghibellines supported the emperors and opposed the pope. To make matters confusing, in Florence there were White *(Bianchi)* and Black *(Neri)* Guelfs. Dante was a White Guelf, until he fell out with them and became a Ghibelline.

Florentines had numerous grounds for dispute, especially financial and religious. There were also rival "Virgil" and "Vergil" spelling camps.

A Famous Florentine
GIOVANNI BOCCACCIO: 1313–75

*B*occaccio claimed to have been born in Paris but probably came from Certaldo, near Florence. He grew up in Florence and was a close friend of Petrarch's and a fierce admirer and defender of Dante's. He studied in Naples, which he called a "great, sinful city." Naples gave him fodder for his rather amoral and celebrated *Decameron, Ten Days,* a series of 100 tales told over 10 days by seven women and three men who fled Florence's 1348 plague. Historians suggest that the book's popularity among Italian society was a testimony to 14th-century licentiousness. Another of his books, *De mulieribus claris, Famous Women,* chronicles the lives of Cleopatra, Zenobia, and Minerva, among others.

Brief Concordance of Boccaccio's *Decameron:*

Basil: day 4, tale 5
Cross-dressing: day 2,
    tale 9; day 7, tale 7
Deception for sexual
    gratification: day 3, tales
    1, 6, 9; day 4, tale 2;
    day 7, tales 1, 2, 3, 4, 6,
    7, 8, 9
Giotto's ugliness: day 6,
    tale 5
Haircuts: day 3, tale 2
Hearts, in cups: day 4, tale 1
Hearts, eating: day 4, tale 9
Pirates: day 2, tales 4, 6

Pregnancy, men: day 9,
    tale 3
Premature burials: day 3,
    tale 8; day 4, tale 10
Relics: day 6, tale 10
Revenge: day 8, tales 7, 8,
    9, 10; day 9, tale 8
Sultans: day 2, tales 7, 9
Thievery, of breeches:
    day 8, tale 5
Thievery, of pigs: day 8,
    tale 6
Wives, turning into
    donkeys: day 9, tale 10

"Isabetta and the Basil": On day four, tale five, in the
Decameron, *Isabetta's brother kills her lover, who comes to her in a dream to tell her where his body is buried. She goes to the spot, digs him up, cuts off his head, and buries it in a pot of basil.*

GIOTTO DI BONDONE

Giotto's reputation as an exquisite painter reached its height in Padua, where his miraculous Cappella degli Scrovegni frescoes can be viewed. In Florence, his paintings are displayed in the Galleria degli Uffizi and at Santa Croce. Giotto began the building of the campanile of the Duomo (also known as Santa Maria del Fiore) in 1334. It is now known as Giotto's Tower (right), even though it was incomplete when he died in 1337.

Giotto's biographer, Giorgio Vasari, depicted the artist as a jokester who once painted such a realistic fly on the nose of a portrait that his reputed teacher, Cimabue, kept trying to brush it off. On another occasion, Vasari reported, when Giotto was painting frescoes in the Castel Nuovo for King Robert of Naples, the king said, " 'Giotto, now that it is so hot, I would put aside my painting for a while if I were you.' And Giotto answered: 'I certainly would too, if I were you.' " The frescoes have since been covered up.

Just where Giotto rests has become a controversy, fueled by the discovery, in 1972, of bones near his supposed tomb during an excavation under the Duomo. "Definitely Giotto," claims one side. "Hogwash," says the other.

Campanile di Giotto
Piazza del Duomo

"Giotto was born to give birth to the art of painting."—Vasari, 1550

Monastero di San Marco
Piazza di San Marco

The *Arrabbiati,* Angry Ones, formed to oppose Savonarola. Think of them as you eat your *spaghetti all'arrabbiata*, angry spaghetti, spiced with hot red pepper. Savonarola's followers were called *Piagnoni,* translated by some as "weepers," by others as "cry-babies."

The Piazza della Signoria was named after Florence's executive council. The piazza was later renamed del Gran' Duca, then dei Priori, and then Nazionale, but is now della Signoria again.

BONFIRE OF THE VANITIES

In 1497 and again in 1498, Florence underwent a massive cleansing of sins, as the Dominican friar Girolamo Savonarola (facing page), who had been made the city's de facto ruler, exhorted both rich and poor to destroy the stuff of vanity: jewels, lace, musical instruments, books, anything that a reform-minded cleric might consider sinful. *Moralisti,* often groups of rabid children, cleared houses of these objects and tossed them onto specially built fires in the Piazze di San Marco and della Signoria.

Savonarola's opponents conspired to have him removed. Pope Alexander VI excommunicated him and forbade him from preaching, but he was so popular that people lined up at the Duomo the day before he was to give a sermon, in order to get good seats.

Then, in May 1498, in a backlash against his fanaticism, an auto-da-fè was arranged for the preacher—an ordeal by fire that would require him to prove his righteousness. The trial, a walk through flames, was thwarted by arguments of procedure, then by a rainstorm. Savonarola's failure to prove his immunity to the flames marked his end. The Signory, city council, voted to banish him; the pope demanded he be sent to Rome for trial. He was, however—along with two disciples—condemned as a heretic and hung, then burned

at the stake in the Piazza della Signoria. A plaque now marks the spot. His ashes were thrown in the Arno to discourage souvenir hunters. Today, it is sometimes possible to have a look in his cell on the first floor of the Museo di San Marco at the monastery of the same name.

Fire and Firenze are still firmly associated. Fireworks are a feature of the Scoppio del Carro, Explosion of the Cart (Easter Sunday), as a fireworks-laden cart placed in front of the Duomo is ignited when a flaming dove-shaped rocket swoops down a wire and crashes into it. Fireworks are also a part of the Festa di San Giovanni (June 24), the kickoff to the medieval football tournament Calcio Storico Fiorentino, celebrating the siege of 1530. The Festa delle Rificolone, Festival of the Lanterns, honoring the Virgin's birthday (September 7), is marked with a lantern-lit procession, as is Befana, Eve of the Epiphany (January 5).

A short inventory of Savonarola's Bonfire of the Vanities: "tapestries and brocades of immodest design, pictures and sculptures held too likely to incite to vice; . . . boards and tables for all sorts of games, playing-cards along with blocks for printing them, dice, and other apparatus for gambling; . . . worldly music-books, and musical instruments in all the pretty varieties . . . masks and masquerading-dresses . . . implements of feminine vanity—rouge-pots, false hair, mirrors, perfumes, powders, and transparent veils intended to provoke inquisitive glances."—George Eliot, *Romola,* 1863

A Famous Florentine
PIERO DI COSIMO: c. 1461–1521

Piero di Cosimo, a Florentine painter who lived during Savonarola's time, favored mythological and allegorical themes. His affinity for the bizarre made him a favorite masquerade decorator. At one Florence carnival, he devised a kind of vehicle of death, hauled by black buffaloes with white-painted faces. On the float was a towering form covered in black cloth, on which stood an immense figure of Death, holding a scythe. Tombs around the edges of the float opened whenever the procession halted, revealing masked men whose black robes were painted as skeletons. At the ghastly bleat of a trumpet, the skeletons emerged, chanting. Other figures of the dead, mounted on bony, cadaverous horses, escorted the float.

According to Vasari, Piero kept to himself. He was nasty to anyone who dared interrupt his work. Neglect of his person and surroundings was one of his most identifiable traits, and he would declare, ad nauseam, that nature was best when it ran wild. His diet was spare, mostly hard-boiled eggs, which he cooked 50 at a time. As a youth he was eccentric; in old age, he was intolerable, reviling doctors and condoning public executions. Apprentices must have sighed in relief when he was found dead at the bottom of his stairs.

His paintings are displayed at Florence's Galleria degli Uffizi and Spedale degli Innocenti.

"[Piero] was sometimes so intent on what he was doing that those who conversed with him were frequently obliged to repeat all they said, for his brain had gone on to other ideas."
—Vasari, on Piero di Cosimo, 1550

Galleria degli Uffizi
Piazza degli Uffizi

Spedale degli Innocenti
Piazza della Santissima Annunziata

SANTA CROCE

This beautiful Gothic church contains the tombs of Michelangelo, Machiavelli, and the poet Vittorio Alfieri. All of Galileo is here except his right-hand middle finger. Dante's monument was erected in 1829, a mere 500 years after he died, showing how long the bitterness about his political affliation with the White Guelfs lasted.

When Stendhal visited Santa Croce and considered the illustrious names, he wrote that the tombs gave him the "desire to be buried." If he could have foreseen that his hero, composer Gioacchino Rossini, would eventually come to rest in this church, he might have made advance arrangements to join him in eternity.

Once you know that between 1284 and 1782 Inquisition tribunals were held in the Minor Refectory, Santa Croce seems rather sinister. Here, astrologers, astronomers, and philosophers were sentenced to exile, imprisonment, or execution for their heretical beliefs. In the case of astronomer Cecco d'Ascoli, who was burned, his censured manuscripts fueled his fire. Those condemned to death were lead along Via de' Malcontenti to "Africa" (Prato della Giustizia), just outside the nearby city wall, where they were executed. The name "Africa" presumably came from its isolation from the city proper.

Basilica di Santa Croce
Cappella de' Pazzi
Piazza di Santa Croce

The dome of the Cappella de' Pazzi is by Filippo Brunelleschi, who also constructed the magnificent dome on the Duomo, Santa Maria del Fiore.

Hotel Casci
Via Cavour 13, near Piazza di San Marco
This hotel was Rossini's home from 1851 to 1855. The composer died in Paris in 1868, but his remains were brought to Florence eight years later. If he had a choice, he'd no doubt prefer to be in Rome, closer to his modern-day angel, mezzo-soprano Cecilia Bartoli.

Excursion from Florence: Arcetri
GALILEO GALILEI: 1564–1642

From 1631, after his run-in with the Inquisition, until his death 11 years later, Galileo Galilei, originally from Pisa, lived at Arcetri, directly south of Florence. It was there in 1638 that he was visited by English poet John Milton, who had been making an extensive Continental tour, seeking out Italy's many literary and scientific scholars.

Star Tower of Galileo
Gioiello Arcetri
Arcetri

Galileo's House
Via Costa di San Giorgio 19

Although Galileo was forced to recant his work and copies of his book *Dialogues on the Ptolemaic and Copernican Systems of the World* were burnt, he never stopped studying the heavens. His Torre del Gallo, Star Tower, became his observatory until his increasing blindness finally deprived him of all sight. Gioiello Arcetri, his villa, still stands but is privately owned.

Most people are aware of Galileo's dedication to the stars and mathematics, but he was also an enthusiastic œnophile who spent so little on food and material goods that he had no compunction about splurging on wine. He also cultivated grapevines.

Before moving to Arcetri, Galileo lived in Florence. His house on the Oltrarno, the left bank, overlooks the Boboli Gardens.

A Famous Florentine
BENVENUTO CELLINI: 1500–1571

*C*ellini was extravagant and vain and, by his own assertions, handsome, brave, talented, and lusty. As an artist, he is best known for his statue of Perseus in the Piazza della Signoria and for a gold salt cellar made for Francesco de' Medici.[2]

To simply call Cellini a Florentine sculptor and goldsmith, however, is to ignore his many other accomplishments, especially his life of excitement. His autobiography is filled with adventures, such as his killing of Charles de Bourbon with his trusty harquebus, a heavy matchlock gun, during the 1527 Sack of Rome. When Cellini was imprisoned in Rome's Castel Sant'Angelo, accused of stealing Pope Paul III's jewels, he escaped, breaking his leg. He reputedly murdered his two-year-old son in front of the boy's mother (he blamed a negligent nurse) and was cured of syphilis by renowned surgeon Berengario da Carpi.

Cellini's Studio: Casa di Ricceri
Via della Pergola 59

His casting of Perseus nearly destroyed his studio, now the Casa di Ricceri, when sparks from the molten bronze set the roof on fire.

2 This salt cellar ended up at Vienna's Kunsthistorisches Museum, from where it was stolen in May 2003. At last word, a ransom was specified, but the museum was not releasing details.

THE ILLUSTRIOUS DEAD

Although visiting the tombs of famous
Florentines is a worthy pastime, their houses,
often still lived in, are even more interesting.

Giovanni Cimabue (c. 1240/50–c. 1302) has
long been considered the father of the Tuscan
school of painting, thanks to Vasari's compli-
mentary biography. Vasari wrote that Borgo
Allegri, Merry Street, was so-called because of
a joyous procession that followed Cimabue's
painting *Ruccellai Madonna* from the artist's
studio to Santa Maria Novella. But scholars
now believe that Cimabue did not paint this
work and attribute it to Duccio of Siena. The
street was likely named Allegri because it was
lined with brothels.

Painter, sculptor, and poet Michelangelo
(1475–1564) bought a house on Via Ghibellina
in 1508, but it was rebuilt in the 17th century.
Michelangelo's nephew turned it into a
museum in 1612, then it was bequeathed to
the city in 1858. Many works of art are displayed here, along with personal effects.

Sculptor Lorenzo Ghiberti (c. 1378–1455)
competed with Filippo Brunelleschi, the
innovative architect of the Duomo's dome,
for the honor of creating two of the three
bronze relief doors of the Duomo Baptistry.
Ghiberti's home on Via Bufalini now houses
two smart hotels.

Casa di Cimabue
Borgo Allegri 5r

Casa Buonarroti
Via Ghibellina 70

Casa di Ghiberti
Via Bufalini 1

FACING PAGE: *Ghiberti's
east door of the Duomo
Baptistry, also called* The
Gates of Paradise, *shows
scenes from the Old
Testament. Ghiberti's*
autoritratto, *self-portrait,
can be found on this door.*

Casa del Sarto
Via Capponi 24,
at Via Giusti
(formerly Via del
Mandorla)

Casa Campigli (House of Machiavelli)
Via dei Guicciardini 16

The House of Amerigo Vespucci
Borgo Ognissanti

FACING PAGE: *Some*
Florentines and their guests:
Top row, from left: Boccaccio,
Walter Savage Landor,
Caterina de' Medici;
center: Elizabeth Barrett
Browning, Giuliano de'
Medici (Duc de Nemours),
Galileo Galilei; bottom:
Michelangelo, Machiavelli,
Frances (Fanny) Trollope.

Painter Andrea del Sarto reputedly died in his Via Capponi house in 1531 in dire poverty. He was both praised and reviled as a remarkable colorist; Ruskin called his *Madonna with St John and St Francis* a "heap of cumbrous nothingness and sickening offensiveness." Many of his Madonnas, modeled after his wife, can be seen at the Pitti Palace and Uffizi Gallery.

When Niccolò Machiavelli wrote *Il principe, The Prince,* around 1513, he could have had no idea it would be used for centuries as a manual on how a cunning ruler should govern. As well as being a writer and historian, he was a negotiator admired for his diplomacy and acute observations. He became an ambassador to Rome, France, and Germany, which gave him an insider's view of Italy's political scene.

World traveler Amerigo Vespucci, after whom America is erroneously named, lived in Borgo Ognissanti until around 1491, when he was sent to Seville by the Medici to work at their shipping business. He became the manager, then was granted Spanish citizenship. He frequently sailed with the ships in the course of his duties and, without a doubt, ended up in South America, probably around the mouth of the Amazon, in 1499, and the Rio Plata, two years later. Cartographer Martin Waldseemüller gave Amerigo's name to what is now South America in 1507. He died in Spain in 1512.

Rooms with a View

Accommodating, cheap, and full of congenial society, Florence was a popular residence for foreigners. It was also a favored place to die, judging from the English expatriates, including poet Elizabeth Barrett Browning, novelist and travel writer Fanny Trollope, and poet Walter Savage Landor, who are buried in the Protestant Cemetery.

Casa Guidi
Via Maggio
Piazza San Felice 1

Browning and her husband, Robert, lived on Via Maggio (now the Browning Institute) from 1846 until her death in 1861. Fanny Trollope, famous for her denunciation of the United States, *Domestic Manners of the Americans,* lived in Villino Trollope in the 1860s until her death in 1863.

Villino Trollope
Piazza dell'Independenzia

Villa Gherardesca
Fiesole, 8 km/5 mi. northeast of Florence

Hotheaded Landor made Italy, and especially Florence, his long-term refuge after being threatened on several occasions with libel. In 1821, he stayed in a palace on Borgo degli Albizi, then quarreled with his landlord and moved to the Villa Castiglione, south of Florence. When his lease expired in 1829, he moved to Villa Gherardesca in nearby Fiesole, bought for him by a friend. He moved to an apartment kept by a former maid of the Brownings on Via Nunziatina, near Casa Guidi, in the early 1860s and lived there until his death in 1864. Of the many foreigners who died in Florence, Landor was one who hung on too long. Infamous for picking fights with the tradesmen who came to his house, he also turned against his own domestics and once threw his cook out a window.

Protestant Cemetery
Piazzale Donatello, near Piazza d'Azeglio

MEDICI POWER

The name Medici is etymologically related to medicine, but no physicians show up in their extensive family tree. Instead, they produced extraordinary despots and patrons of the arts. They became extremely wealthy, as traders in cloth, spice, and real estate, and, through usury, as bankers to popes. Their power pushed them into a fierce rivalry with the already established merchant families, the Pazzi, Strozzi, and Albizzi.

Legendery Medici names include Cosimo the Elder and Piero the Gouty, but Lorenzo the Magnificent (above) stands out among them. A poet and connoisseur, Lorenzo used diplomacy rather than warfare to expand territory and secure alliances. But he clashed with Pope Sixtus IV, a profligate spender. The Medici were the pope's bankers, but Sixtus

Lorenzo il magnifico
1449–92
Lorenzo's great contributions to Italy's literary and plastic arts raised him above other rulers, though in most other ways he carried on like any other tyrant, behaving immorally, interfering in private affairs, and maintaining a legion of spies. A contemporary noted, however, that if Florence was to have a tyrant, she couldn't have a "better or more pleasant one." Lorenzo survived several assassination attempts and died of natural causes.

The Pazzi

The Pazzi counted knights of the First Crusades among their ancestors. They were influential bankers and owned numerous businesses and properties, including the sumptuous Pazzi Palace, now housing the Banca di Firenze.

Their failed coup against the Medici saw the downfall of their fortunes: family assets were confiscated, they were forced to change their name, and all depictions of their coat of arms were eradicated. As well, streets carrying the name Pazzi were renamed, and Pazzi women were forbidden to marry.

Palazzo Pazzi

Borgo degli Albizi

borrowed a considerable sum of money from the Pazzi, who told him that Lorenzo had tried to interfere with the transaction. The pope then switched his banking to the Pazzi and joined with them to dislodge the Medici.

On 26 April 1478, after months of planning, the Pazzi made their move. With the help of priests and henchmen, they attacked brothers Lorenzo and Giuliano de' Medici during Mass in the Duomo. Lorenzo escaped, but Giuliano (background) was stabbed a frenzied 19 times by several attackers and died of his wounds. Ringleader Jacopo de' Pazzi, flanked by some 100 mercenaries, tried to pull off a coup but, finding no support from Florentines, fled. The conspirators were rounded up one by one and brought back dead or alive, whole or in bits.

Jacopo was captured, tortured, then hanged in the Piazza della Signoria. He was buried in the family crypt at Santa Croce, but after four days of rain, farmers were convinced that God disapproved of his impious burial and predicted a failure of their crops. Jacopo was then pulled from his tomb and reburied outside city walls. When demons were reported in the vicinity, he was again yanked from his grave. His remains were flung into the Arno but not before being dragged ignominiously around the town, the noose still around his neck, by an unruly mob of boys.

SAN LORENZO AND THE MEDICI

San Lorenzo hides a terrifying tale. In 1791, Ferdinand III, Hapsburgian Grand Duke of Tuscany, had all 49 Medici corpses interred in the Medici Chapel here, shoved into a subterranean vault. The door was locked and the remains forgotten until 1857, when the keepers of the church, embarrassed by the poor treatment of these notables, decided to restore them to the chapel.

When they opened the door to the vault, they were revolted by the miasma of putrefaction. They discovered that someone, robbers perhaps, had been there first, or the deceased had been battling among themselves. Rats scuttled in and out of shattered coffins. The bones of those not embalmed had been flung about. Those who had been preserved gazed upon their discoverers with dark and maniacal expressions on their wizened faces. Rings had been torn off fingers, and bracelets and necklaces off wrists and necks; gold thread had been yanked off velvet dresses. The bones of *condottiere* Giovanni delle Bande Nere (Giovanni of the Black Bands) rattled about loosely in the armor in which he had been buried, and the visor was rusted shut. His remains were extracted from their metal sarcophagus, revealing the cause of his death: his right leg had been badly amputated.

Cappelle Medicee
Basilica di San Lorenzo
Piazza di Madonna degli Aldobrandini

San Lorenzo, a fourth-century church, became, after many additions and changes, the Medici church. Brunelleschi and Michelangelo were commissioned by the Medici to rebuild portions of it.

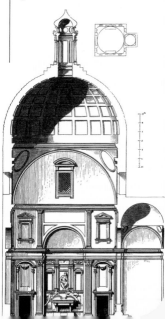

The original recipe called for jasmine, cinnamon, vanilla, ambergris or amber, and musk. A version published after Cosimo's death specified 5 kg/10 lb. cocoa, mixed with "a sufficient quantity" of jasmine petals, 4 kg/8 lb. sugar, 90 g/3 oz. vanilla, 185 g/6 oz. cinnamon, and 2½ g/⅛ oz. (or 2 scruples) ambergris. The mixture was heated, turned out onto a heated stone, and kneaded.

THE GRAND DUKE'S JASMINE CHOCOLATE

Jasmine was cultivated in Florence by Cosimo III (1642–1723), who had been given a *Jasmine sambac,* Indian jasmine, by the Portuguese. It became known as the Grand Duke's Jasmine, and Cosimo forbade anyone to take a cutting of his beloved flower. The fragrant petals were added to a recipe for chocolates already heady with the aroma of ambergris. This updated version uses semisweet dark chocolate and omits the ambergris.

Filling: Boil 60 ml/¼ cup whipping cream, set aside to cool slightly, then stir in 60 g/1 cup fresh jasmine petals. (Do not use yellow jasmine, as it is poisonous.) Let steep for 5 minutes, then strain out the petals. Add the cream, 2 tbsp. unsalted butter, and 1 tsp. vanilla extract to 185 g/6 oz. melted chocolate. Cool to room temperature, then scoop into a pastry cone.

Coating: Temper 315 g/10 oz. chocolate (consult cookbooks for this process, which is too lengthy to cover here). Using a plastic truffleform, coat each mold with a layer of chocolate, and let set. Drop a fresh jasmine blossom into each mold and pipe in the filling. Level off, cover with tempered chocolate, and chill for 20 minutes. Makes 25 to 40 chocolates, depending on the mold size. The jasmine becomes tasteless after three days, so eat these chocolates quickly.

GELATI

Although Florence no more deserves to be known for its gelato than, say, Rome or Milan (try Palermo or Turin for the best), it still commands the distinction of being the source of Italian ice cream as we know it today.[3]

Florence's prominence dates from 1565, when Bernardo Buontalenti concocted an ice cream fantasy for a Medici dinner party, attended by Caterina de' Medici, who subsequently took the idea of frozen deserts with her to France when she married the soon-to-be King Henry II. Buontalenti's icy confections, combined with an earlier discovery of saltpeter's ability to quickly freeze liquids, meant that gelati soon became available to everyone, and Florence *gelatai,* ice-cream makers, instantly flourished.

3 Some "epicurious" historians credit Marco Polo for bringing the idea of ice cream, made from ice, back from China in the 14th century. Others suggest that it was known to the Romans. Nero reportedly ate mountain snow flavored with honey, spices, and fruit. Sorbet appeared in Sicily with the Arabs, as Mt Etna snow mixed with juice.

Bernardo Buontalenti
c. 1531–1608
Architect, engineer, artist, set designer, and a maker of automata, Buontalenti was commissioned by Francesco de' Medici to contribute to the design of the Boboli Gardens (his grottoes were based on Ovid's *Metamorphoses*), the Galleria degli Uffizi (after the death of Vasari, the original architect), the facade of Santa Trinità, and the Palazzo Nonfinito, among others.

The Tuscan saying *"Si stava meglio quando si stava peggio"* (We were better off when we were worse off) suggests that Tuscans prefer a meager diet.

Gelati a casa in 5 minuti

Si possono fare da se stessi, con ii parmjo di ghiaccio, usando la nuova e perfetta macchina americana **" VELOCE ,,** ad espansione centrifuga. Costruita fortemente in metallo è di durata illimitata e di funzionamento così facile che anche un fanciullo può usarla. Si restituisce il denaro se la macchina non fa gelati in circa 5 minuti.

La Veloce macchina sufficiente per 4 ge lati per volta costa soltanto L.. **2,90** per 8 gelati L. **3,60** e per 12 a 16 gelati L. **6**. **Gratis** ai Clienti *Ricettario moderno* per fare i migliori gelati, sorbetti, gramolate, ecc., con risparmio dl'80 010. Inviare relativo importo alla

Premiata Ditta FRASCOGNA - Via Orivolo, 35 - Firenze

Science Museums

*M*ost of the natural history specimens in the amazing Zoological Museum and Observatory came from the collections of the Medici. Stuffed and pickled animals (including Grand Duke Pietro Leopoldo's hippopotamus), hunting trophies from the Count of Turin, and an elephant-skin sofa are a few of the treasures, but most people come to wince at the wax anatomies.

Created mostly in the 18th century by Clemente Susini and Felice Fontana, the anatomical figures in this museum reveal, in fine detail, the veins, arteries, nerves, bones, and muscles of the human body. Certain pathologies are also exhibited. They are not for the faint of heart.

Traveler Joseph Forsyth saw this *gabinetto fisico,* physical cabinet, in 1802. He wasn't so much shocked by the anatomy but that "this awful region, which should be sacred to men of science, is open to all. Nay, the very apartment where the gravid uterus and its processes lie unveiled is a favourite lounge of the ladies, who criticise aloud all the mysteries of sex."

Mariana Starke wrote in her 1839 *Guide to Europe* that the anatomical display, especially of the plague, was "so painfully fine that few persons can bear to examine it." The models she saw were probably prepared by Abbot Gaetano Zumbo (1656–1701). Horrifyingly lifelike, they were commissioned by Cosmo II and can still be seen.

Museo Zoologico la Specola
Via Romana 17

Museo di Storia della Scienza
Piazza dei Giudici 1

Also for the science minded is the History of Science Museum. Here you'll find Galileo's right-hand middle finger[4] and one of his telescopes. There are also clocks, automata, pumps, anatomical models, armillary spheres, and optical devices.

4 The rest of Galileo is in the Novice's Chapel, Santa Croce.

Arezzo. Via Vittorio Emanuele

Arezzo

Aretina: a breed of ponies

Aretino: a kind of crystal vase, made in Arezzo; a native of Arezzo

 Etruscany

The kingdoms of Etruria were Arezzo, Veii, Caere (Cerveteri), Falerii, Tarquinii, Volci, and Volsinii, all north of Rome; and Clusium (Chiusi), Cortona, Perusia (Perugia), Volaterrae (Volterra), Populonia, and Russellae (Grosseto) in Tuscany and Umbria.

PREVIOUS PAGE: *Via Vittorio Emanuele, Arezzo.* BACKGROUND: *The Etruscan alphabet, as designed by Bodoni.*

ETERNALLY OVERSHADOWED BY its northern neighbor, Florence, Arezzo sheltered many exiled Florentines, such as Dante, who never balked at a chance to insult their temporary haven. Arezzo's most famous offspring left to find more fertile pastures, but the city nevertheless draws lovers of bric-a-brac and students of frescoes and Etruscans.

There's a prosperous air here, which derives largely from Arezzo's fortunes as a center of gold jewelry. Complacency and comfort are evident in its streets. Liveliness breaks out in pockets: lunchtime at the *caffè*, weekends during the monthly antique market, occasionally in the lineup to see the Piero frescoes. The relaxed mood draws you in, and you imagine living here, but after the antique dealers fold up their tables, the church door closes, and you've had lunch, you move on, just like everyone else.

Having been heavily bombed and rebuilt after WWII, Arezzo has few traces of its distant past as the Etruscan kingdom of Arretium. What remains—a modest amphitheater and a few tombs; the distinctive *vasi aretini*, Aretine vases, made of terra-cotta; and bronze tools and weapons—give little idea of its former status as a powerful Etruscan center. However, Arezzo has remnants of the fabulous animals, like the Chimera, that made up the Etruscan menagerie.

THE CHIMERA

The lion's head on the bronze Chimera of Arezzo (left) roars impotently at the insolent goat erupting from its back. A serpent's tail (not visible here) adds to the insult, but what all this means remains a mystery. Dating to the fourth century B.C., the Chimera was unearthed in the 1550s.

The Chimera joins other members of the Etruscan menagerie found at numerous sites throughout central Italy: fabulous animals such as the hippocampus at Tarquinia, described by D. H. Lawrence as a horse with the tail of a fish, and a sinuous yet stately bronze merman at Perugia. Scarabs and beetles, onto which designs have been engraved, and a host of satyrs, sirens, centaurs, and gorgons can be seen at Cerveteri, Volterra, and nearby Cortona.

Although Arezzo is liberally adorned with reproduction Chimeras, including an impressive statue near the train station, the original is in Florence's Museo Archeologico. Other Etruscan finds—mirrors, jewelry, bronzes, and vases—are at Arezzo's Archaeological Museum named after Caius Cilnius Maecenas, an Aretine descendant of Etruscan rulers and a friend of Augustus's.

Museo Archeologico Mecenate
Via Margaritone 10

"You mustn't tip the guide, as he is gratuitous."—Notice at Caere (Cerveteri), quoted by D. H. Lawrence

LEFT: *An Etruscan gorgon.*
BELOW: *Etruscan winged figure.*
BACKGROUND: *Etruscan mirror.*

Famous Aretines

Arezzo's citizens of note tended to make their names elsewhere. Three of the most famous, Petrarch, Pietro Aretino, and Giorgio Vasari, barely lived in the place. The poet Petrarch spent so little time in Arezzo that he was called "Arezzo's accidental child." His former home is now a museum, housing the Petrarch Academy.

Casa di Petrarca
Accademia Petrarca di
Lettere, Arti e Scienze
Via dell'Orto 28a

Casa Aretino
Via XX Settembre 37

Casa Vasari
Via XX Settembre 55

Guido d'Arezzo
c. 991–1050
Possibly the most forgotten famous Aretine, composer and choirmaster Guido standardized the musical scale. A monument to him stands in Arezzo's Piazza Guido Monaco.

Aretino (1492–1556), who blackmailed the wealthy by hinting at their misdeeds in his poetry, became known as "the scourge of princes." His letters, poems, and comedies still seem outrageously ribald. Popes Leo X and Clement VII, both Medicis, were his patrons. Charles V paid him a "handsome pension" to refrain from slander. From Charles's enemy, Francis I, Aretino received even more largess. After being stabbed in Rome for some vitriolic pasquinades, he went to Venice, where his talents earned him the name *divino*. He raised his daughters Adria and Austria there and made friends with Titian. Fittingly, he is said to have died laughing at a joke.

Vasari (1511–74) was an architect and Mannerist painter who worked mostly in Florence under the patronage of the powerful Medici. Also an avid historian, he collected facts and legends about such artists as Giotto, Raphael, and Botticelli in his influential chronicle of artists, *The Lives of the Most Excellent Italian Architects, Painters, and Sculptors* (1550). Examples of his own art can be seen at his Arezzo house.

FIERA ANTIQUARIA

Reliquaries anyone? Or how about a fragment of a 19th-century plaster cast of a 15th-century likeness of Cosimo de' Medici dressed as a Roman emperor? It seems as though the contents of every attic and cellar in Tuscany have been strewn about the streets and piazze of central Arezzo, and all items are for sale. Paintings, columns, dolls, Tombola games, copperplate engravings, postcards, whatever might appeal to the packrat's lusting soul can be found here. The antiques market attracts more than a thousand dealers and is held on the first weekend of every month.

During the first weekend of September, however, the Piazza Grande gives way to the Giostra del Saracino, the Joust of the Saracens, fought between the four districts of the city.

Vocabolario mercatino
Aggeggio: trifle, worthless thing
Anticaglia: collectibles; *antichità:* antiques
Caro: pricey; *è troppo caro:* it's too expensive
Cianfrusaglia: bric-a-brac
Quanto costa questa?: how much does this cost?
Rigattiere: second-hand clothes dealer
Ristretto: as in *ditemi il ristretto di questo articolo:*
    tell me what's your lowest price on this item
Sconto: discount; *mi fa lo sconto?:* will you make
    me a deal?

Other notable antiques markets:

Rome
Porta Portese
Via Portuense, Trastevere
Sunday mornings, many dealers

Lucca
In the streets around the Duomo
Third weekend of every month, about 250 dealers

Naples
Fiera Antiquaria Napoletana
Parco Villa Communale
Third weekend of every month, except August, about 300 dealers

Chiesa di San Francesco
Piazza San Francesco

"Truly unhappy are
those who, after
labouring over their
studies to give pleasure
to others and to leave
behind a name for
themselves, are not
permitted either by
sickness or death to
bring to perfection
the works they have
begun."—Vasari, on
Piero della Francesca,
1550

THE PIERO FRESCOES

The slow and meticulous Piero della Francesca
spent 14 years painting the frescoes of the legend
of the True Cross in San Francesco. He took
over from Bicci di Lorenzo, who died just after
starting in 1452, and worked on
them until 1466. The frescoes are
based on Jacopo da Voragine's
Legenda aurea, Golden Legend.
His version of this story
recounts how the wood for
the cross came from a branch
of the Tree of Knowledge, which had been
given to Seth, Adam's son, to plant in his dead
father's mouth. Solomon used the tree to build
a bridge, but the Queen of Sheba, recognizing
the holy nature of the wood, refused to tread
upon it and warned Solomon that it would
cause the destruction of the Jews. Solomon
buried it, but as the time for Jesus's crucifixion
drew close, it resurfaced and was used to make
the cross.

Piero's first known work was the *Resurrection
of Christ,* in Sansepolcro.[1] He also painted
portraits of the Duke of Urbino, Federigo da
Montefeltro, and Battista Sforza and wrote
treatises on arithmetic, geometry, and painting.

1 Piero was born in Sansepolcro, now best known as the
headquarters of Buitoni pasta.

PERUGIA

1:10.000

Metri

0 100 200 300 400 500

Porta S. Susanna

Cupa

Teatro d. Pavone

Umberto I

Baglioni

Garibaldi

Tribunali

Porta S. Margher

Manicomio Margherita

Pia. Elce

Mattatoio

Università

S. Sostino

Pia. del Bula

Pia. S. Antonio

Bersaglieri

Cimitero

FONTE-NUOVO

Mad. Mte Luce

Perugia

Perugino: native of, or relating to, Perugia

La scala mobile

An escalator runs between the lower-level bus and train stations and the upper town's Piazza Italia. It cuts through Rocca Paolina, once a papal fortress built by Paul III in 1540. When Perugia joined the Risorgimento in 1860, above-surface areas of the fort were destroyed. The remaining underground chambers and passageways offer as modern a view of the medieval as you are ever likely to find.

PREVIOUS PAGE: *Perugia, 1909.*

TOWNS IN LANDLOCKED Umbria are isolated and inward looking. Perugia is no exception, in spite of the large population of foreign students at its university. But don't expect a cold welcome, especially ladies. If past visits are any indication, the gentlemen of Perugia are most anxious to make your acquaintance and will soon offer to take you boating on nearby Lake Trasimeno.

Not everyone has been given hospitality, however. Since its founding as an Etruscan city in the sixth century B.C., Perugia has shown a marked antipathy to visitors and has fought, in vain, Romans, Goths, and Lombards. It reluctantly submitted to the pope in the ninth century, but in 1375, Pope Gregory XI, incensed by the town's disobedience, nearly excommunicated it. In 1520, Leo X had Gianpaolo Baglioni, from one of Perugia's leading families, beheaded. In 1780, during a revolt against the papacy, the statue of Julius III was removed from Piazza del Papa and stowed in a tavern cellar until tempers cooled. Nonetheless, popes sought asylum within its walls, and three are buried here.

Given the intensity of emotions in Perugia, it's fitting that flagellants, scourgers of the flesh, originated here in the 1260s, and that it is infamous for the poison *aquetta* (juice of pork that has been rubbed with arsenic).

LEFT: *A flagellant.*
BACKGROUND: *Detail of an Etruscan antefix, Museo Archeologico Nazionale dell'Umbria.*

Perugia's narrow and oppressive lanes feel haunted. Some of the houses lining them are still equipped with doors for the dead, though they are now blocked up. These *porte,* small, discreet openings, answered the tricky question of how to remove a body that had been brought to its own house to be watched and mourned over, without letting its ghost return. The *porte* were just large enough for a coffin to slide through and were sealed up once the body was gone. The logic behind this was that spirits would only try to get in the way that they had left.

If the claustrophobic city and its violent past becomes too much, you are never far from a gate from which you'll be treated to unparalleled views of the countryside, no matter the direction you turn. As Henry James said after a stay of one week, you can never get "enough of the View."

LA BATTAGLIA DEI SASSI

In the 16th century, Perugia's Campo di Battagliai was the site of the Battle of the Stones, which pitted *condotierri,* mercenaries, against *i popoli,* the people. The two sides took their positions, one on the square, the other just below. Each team had *armati,* combatants, and *laciatori,* an

Gianpaolo Baglioni
d. 1520
For a violent and treasonous attack on his family, Gianpaolo Baglioni, the "bloody and licentious despot of Perugia," ordered the massacre of more than 100 rebels. Their heads decorated his palazzo walls, and their portraits, painted in fresco, hung upside down beside them.

advance crew armed with stones. The object of the game was to hurl the stones at the opposing team and hold or take the square (depending on the starting position). However, there were no rules. Any projectile could be used, and anyone could join either side. It wasn't uncommon for a dozen dead to be hauled off the field when the final whistle blew.

PERUGINO

The sweet paintings of Perugino (c. 1450–1523), Perugia's most famous artist, are welcome antidotes to Perugia's violent history. Perugino was introduced to painting as a painter's apprentice. He couldn't resist the pull of Florence but was so poor when he first moved there that he slept in a chest. Dread of poverty drove him to work on anything, just for money. His doe-eyed Madonnas pleased the wealthy, and his paintings were often sold and resold within his lifetime at several times their original value. Perugino feared for his livelihood when Michelangelo appeared, and behaved so badly toward the young artist that Michelangelo called him a "blockhead." In Perugia, his paintings can be seen at the San Agostino, San Severo, San Pietro, and San Domenico churches, and in the Galleria Nazionale dell'Umbria.

"Learn to trust honest men who never deceive those who trust them but who know how very well, if they wish, to deceive suspicious men."—Perugino, quoted by Vasari, 1550

BACKGROUND: *Detail of Perugino's* Madonna and Child.

Pisa

Pisano: native of Pisa

"If Pisa be the seventh wonder of the world in right of its Tower, it may claim to be, at least, the second or third in right of its beggars."—Charles Dickens, *Pictures from Italy,* 1846

"Pisa is a blend of big city and small town, of urban and rural folk—a mixture so romantic that I have never seen anything like it."—Giacomo Leopardi, 1827

BACKGROUND: *Map of Pisa, 1885, and plan of the Duomo.*
PREVIOUS PAGE: *The Campo dei Miracoli and the Leaning Tower, c. 1905.*

THE DAILY CIRCUS conducted around the edges of Pisa's Campo dei Miracoli obscures almost every other feature of this once-great city. The hordes of tourists having a good time propping up the Torre Pendente, Leaning Tower (in more ways than one), have shifted the city's focus away from its lively center, its 9 km/6 mi. of ramparts, and its university.

Pisa owes its former power to its position on the Arno and its access to the sea. Its navy was kept busy by a plentiful supply of enemies: Luccans and Sicilian Saracens; and rivals: Genoese, Venetians, and Amalfians. Pisa's coffers were filled by the booty of the vanquished. And through the city's involvement in the Second Crusades, Pisans reaped profit from commerce with the East.

Pisa's immense wealth financed such spectacular buildings as the Duomo and Baptistry. The *camposanto,* cemetery, is reputedly covered with holy soil brought from Jerusalem by some 53 Pisan ships returning from the Crusades.

Aside from the grand buildings, little remains of Pisa's former glory, but if you tear yourself away from the Leaning Tower, you'll find that a beautifully laid out and flourishing city has been hiding behind your back all the while.

THE GHOSTS OF LANFRANCHI

In 1821, Byron, his mistress, Countess Teresa Gamba Guiccioli, and her husband, Alessandro, lived in the Palazzo Lanfranchi on the Lungarno. It had been rented for him by the Shelleys, who were living in Tre Palazzi di Chiesa. Byron, blessed with an active imagination (he adored the gothic tales of English novelist Mrs Radcliffe), was pleased to find the place haunted:

> I have got here into a famous old feudal palazzo, on the Arno, large enough for a garrison, with dungeons below and cells in the walls, and so full of *ghosts* that the learned Fletcher (my valet) has begged leave to change his room, and then refused to occupy his *new* room, because there were more ghosts there than in the other. It is quite true that there are most extraordinary noises (as in all old buildings), which have terrified the servants so as to incommode me extremely. There is one place where people were evidently *walled up,* for there is but one possible passage, broken through the wall, and then meant to be closed again upon the inmate. The house belonged to the Lanfranchi family (the same mentioned by Ugolino in his dream, as his persecutor with Sismondi), and has had a fierce owner or two in its time.

Palazzo Lanfranchi

Now the Palazzo Toscanelli and State Archives
Lungarno Mediceo 30

In Pisa, Byron gave extravagant dinners on Wednesday nights for men only, usually Percy Bysshe Shelley, Shelley's friend Edward Williams and cousin Thomas Medwin, and Irish expatriate John Taafe, Jr. The gathering was called "Lord Byron's Pistol Club," named for their pastime of target practicing.

A Famous Pisan
COUNT UGOLINO DELLA GHERARDESCA: d. 1288

Ugolino, de facto ruler of Pisa, was declared a traitor and exiled. In revenge, he and his supporters joined Florence and, with that city's help, returned to rule Pisa with even more power. Again accused of treason, he and his three sons were locked in what became known as the "Tower of Famine," where they died of starvation.

Torre della Famine
Demolished 1655
Piazza dei Cavalieri

"That sinner from the savage meal his mouth
Uplifted, wiping it upon the hair
Of the head which he'd wasted from behind."
—Ugolino, eternally devouring the former Archbishop Ruggieri, *The Inferno,* Canto 33

BACKGROUND: The Last Judgment and Hell, *detail, by Orcagna, 14th century, Camposanto, Pisa.*

Dante relegated Ugolino to the *Inferno,* and Heinrich Wilhelm von Gerstenberg wrote the tragic play, *Ugolino* (1768), based on the count's life, in which son Francesco escapes while Ugolino and his remaining two sons fantasize about food. Later, the dead bodies of Ugolino's wife and Francesco, who had been poisoned, are brought into the tower in coffins. Ugolino, delirious, murders his second son, then takes his own life, leaving the last son to starve to death.

German traveler Wilhelmine Buchholz reviewed the play, which she claimed to have seen performed in Pisa, and in which:

all the torments of death by famine are depicted . . . The piece is never played to the end, because when the youngest son in his turn begins to die, and moans that his stomach seemed to be sitting on his shoulders, then the spectators in the gallery are so moved to pity, that they throw sausages and rolls to the poor boy, upon which the piece is stopped.

CONDOTTIERI

Pisa's land wars were fought with the aid of *condottieri,* mercenary leaders of armed bands known as *compagnie di ventura,* companies of adventure. *Condottieri* were found throughout Europe but, in Italy, they took on almost mythical status. Many accumulated great wealth, and some became dukes. They were consummate businessmen, insisting on written contracts and full payments, and they were usually given a *condotta in aspetto,* a retainer. In return, they fought fiercely—though most often in territorial skirmishes rather than major battles—and were loyal to their employers as long as they were paid.

Englishman Sir John Hawkwood, also known as Giovanni Acuto, was one of the more audacious *condottieri.* During the late 14th century, he and his Compagnia Bianca, White Company, fought Florence for Pisa, Pisa and Florence for Milan, Arezzo for Perugia, and, lastly, Pisa for Florence. He aided the popes in their battle against the Visconti and took on Bologna for the Church. When he died, Florence went into mourning, and his funeral ceremony halted all activity in the city. His ashes were sent to England. His portrait by Uccello is in the Duomo in Florence.

Condottiere, from *condurre,* conducting, supplying *Condotte,* contracts

Buli: "professional assassins, who, as late as 1775, would hire out their services as required."—Stendhal, 1818

"If a prince holds on to his state by means of mercenary armies, he will never be stable or secure, for they are disunited, ambitious, without discipline, disloyal; they are brave among friends; among enemies they are cowards."
—Machiavelli, *The Prince,* 1532

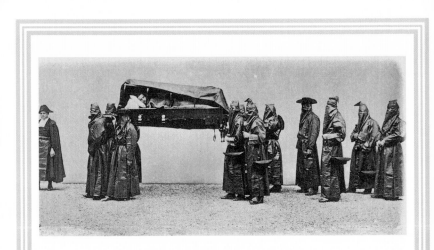

Arciconfraternità della Misericordia

$\mathcal{T}$he Brothers of the Misericordia, or Mercy (above), is a long-enduring religious organization devoted to taking the sick to hospital and to removing the dead. One of their fund-raising processions in Pisa nearly put Wilhelmine Buchholz into an early grave.

Dear Fritz:
Here I am in Pisa. Let me tell you what happened yesterday, while contemplating that rickety thing they call the Tower of Pisa . . . I saw a horrible apparition before me . . . I fled from the spot with a loud shriek of terror, for I believed firmly that Satan in bodily form had come to fetch me and boil me down along with the other souls in the Campo Santo in pitch and sulphur. "Keep away from me, or I shall scratch!" I shrieked. It pushed nearer notwithstanding, and when it had reached my immediate vicinity, it held a sort of collecting box towards me. "Good gracious!" I exclaimed, "since when has money been collected for hell?"—Love, Wilhelmine

ROMA

Roma

Romanamente: in the
Roman way

Romanesco: Roman
dialect

Romanismo: idiom of
Roman dialect

Alla romana: each
paying his share

"Rome is a world,
and it would take
years to become a
true citizen of it. How
lucky those travellers
are who take one
look and leave."
—Goethe, *Italian
Journey,* 1786–88

PREVIOUS PAGE: *The villa
of Livia, wife of Emperor
Augustus, in Rome.*
BACKGROUND: *Rome,
1874.*

THE BEST WAY TO ARRIVE in Rome,
whether you are coming by plane,
train, or car, is via Federico Fellini and his
movie, *Roma.* If this chaotic introduction
appeals to you, then you're ready to explore
the city that functions—as Fellini showed so
well—like a massive, pulsating body, made up
of a head, a stomach, a heart, and a mouth.

Rome's head, the Capitoline, is one of seven
hills that radiates from its belly button, the
Umbilicus Urbis Romæ, in the Forum. It is
said that this hill was named Mons Capitolinus,
Mountain of the Head, when a still-bloody
human head was dug up in the course of
 building the Temple of Jupiter in
535 B.C. At the sight of this omen,
Etruscan soothsayers predicted that
Rome would be the head of Italy,
which meant, at that time, the head of the
world. The sentiment persisted; a 16th-century
map in the Vatican Library shows the city as
just that, the *caput orbis.*

Moving on to Rome's stomach, you find
markets overflowing with every manner of
food and wine because, luckily for the visitor,
all of Italy feeds Rome. In the city's *trattorie,
osterie,* and *ristoranti,* eating isn't a function of
necessity, but a pleasure to be anticipated and
savored. *Saltimbocca,* jump in the mouth, *coda
alla vaccinara,* oxtail stew slaughterhouse-worker

style, *pizza capricciosa,* pizza by whim— the stranger the menu sounds, the more rewarding it is.

Rome's heart, its many churches, museums, and galleries, is but a step away. This heart is filled to the brim with the art and artifacts of an enor-

mous passion for love, war, and God. Don't look just at the treasures contained in these marvelous edifices; the buildings are artworks in themselves and, if emptied, would still inspire awe.

All around you is Rome's mouth, the conversations that are conducted with rich, sonorous voices from dawn until long after darkness descends. Even statues tucked in out-of-the-way piazze are reputed to talk. Adding to this rumble is uncontrollable traffic, amplified by the cobblestones and echoing up narrow streets. Rome wants to be heard, and heard it is! Rome never shuts up, and it's fascinating to listen to its many stories.

For a body such as Rome, where are the *gabinetti,* toilets? By law, *caffè* must accommodate the bladder distressed. Aside from these facilities, the toilet situation seems not to have improved since at least 1802, when Joseph Forsyth, noting their absence, pointed out that more than 140 public conveniences existed in the time of the Roman Republic. An Italian friend of Stendhal's thought that the surplus of toilets in England made one want to go all the time. The *Guide practique Conty* (c. 1930), concerned about facilities, gave locations for WCs in its city directory; Rome had seven.

Domitian (Titus Flavius Domitianus)

A.D. 51–96

Emperor Domitian was such a blood-thirsty despot that it was no surprise, even to himself, that he was murdered. His paranoia drove him to walk in a gallery lined with reflective stone, so he could see all around him. In spite of his precautions, he was stabbed to death. Vanity was another vice: when he prematurely went bald, he wrote a manual on hair care.

ABOVE AND RIGHT: *Nero Claudius Caesar Drusus Germanicus and his second wife, Poppaea Sabina.*
BACKGROUND: *Domitian.*

ROMAN EMPERORS

Historians make much of Rome's emperors, good or evil, starting with Julius Caesar (actually self-proclaimed "dictator for life"), who was stabbed to death because of his lust for power. His successor was the first emperor, Augustus, then the position briefly became hereditary, but the line disintegrated, as all decent contenders were poisoned. Of those who succeeded Augustus, Nero (A.D. 37–68) has attracted the most rancor, but could it be his wives' fault, as traveler Wilhelmine Buchholz suggests?

Nero's first wife, Octavia, is said to have been very good for her days, but her fault was this—she did not know how to manage Nero. The consequence was that Nero led a most dreadful life, often returned neither by day nor night to his home, and made the acquaintance of a certain Poppaea Sabina, whom he also married after causing Octavia to be executed. Now this Sabina was just the very

worst sort of wife for a man like Nero. Her toilettes alone were sufficient to ruin him! The mules that bore her about were shod with golden shoes, and the milk of five hundred asses was provided daily to supply her bath. And this only for the sake of her complexion. With such a wife Nero must of course take to bad courses, for when a woman begins by bathing in milk, what will she drink with her coffee afterwards?

ABOVE: *"Nero as a parrot," being driven by "Locusta as a cricket," from a wall painting at Pompeii.*

THE VAULT OF HEAVEN

The Pantheon, built in A.D. 125 over a temple dating to 27 B.C., is one of Rome's most enduring and well-preserved ancient monuments. But, unless you've come at a quiet moment, you'll need to go inside to appreciate it fully. When it's busy, and it often is, you'll be stepping around and over blue tarps spread out across the column-studded porch. Belonging to street vendors from Saigon, Fuzhou, and Nigeria, these tarps are covered with the latest in binoculars, whirlygigs, tripods, good-luck charms, and Guci [*sic*] handbags.

Once inside, you'll be astonished by its size (the walls are 7 m/22 ft. thick), its finish (of marble and porphyry), and its dome (with an equal height and diameter of 46 m/142 ft.). The dome, or the "brazen canopy," as Erasmus Darwin called it, is an engineering marvel for its size alone, but the oculus, the open hole at

The Pantheon
Piazza della Rotonda

Raphael, Raffaello Sanzio
1483–1520
Raphael is buried in the Pantheon, but it's unclear when his body was brought there. In 1828, Stendhal reported that the artist's skull was in San Luca, also in Rome, and that, from it, he could tell that Raphael was short.

The Pantheon is also known as Santa Maria Rotonda, which could be translated as St Mary the Round or even St Mary the Chubby, taking a cue from Venice's Santa Maria Formosa, Church of the Buxom Mary.

Umberto D.

Those who've seen Vittoria de Sica's great movie *Umberto D.* will visit the Pantheon with an eye to spotting a small, intelligent terrier that goes by the name of Flag. He will be near the entrance, holding his master's often-brushed fedora in his mouth.

Interior of the Pantheon, c. 1850.

its top is fascinating. How can it be left open? Doesn't it let in the weather? Birds? It does, and it also illuminates the interior with a sublime glow, one of many things that makes this edifice so stunning. From the floor far below, the oculus looks tiny; it is, in fact, 9.5 m/29 ft. in diameter.

Originally intended as a temple—the name means "very sacred"—the Pantheon became a Christian edifice in 609 and houses the tombs of Raphael and Vittorio Emanuele II.

Egypt in Rome Itinerary

*R*omans launched the Egyptian craze in the first century B.C., when they started importing obelisks. With a total of 13 still standing, and as many as 30 lying buried and broken, the city seems to have more of the monoliths than Egypt. They were first brought back by Augustus, as if he were taking revenge on Cleopatra for having seduced Julius Caesar and Mark Antony. Others were imported by Hadrian, Constantine, and Mussolini (though his, the obelisk of Axum from Ethiopia, has been returned). Yet others were made by Romans, inspired by the Egyptian originals. Almost none stands where it was first placed. Pope Sixtus V did a massive *renovatio* in 1586–89 and had many obelisks moved to significant religious locations. Pius VI had others moved between 1789 and 1792.

Piazza di San Giovanni in Laterano

This 15th-century-B.C. red granite obelisk from the Temple of Ammon in Thebes was brought to Rome by Constantius II in A.D. 357 and placed in the Circus Maximus, where it was found, lying in three pieces, in 1587. It was then moved to where it stands today. It is Rome's tallest obelisk at 469 m/154 ft., including pedestal, and weighs about 390 tonnes/430 tons.

Piazza del Popolo

This obelisk (shown in the background) has a four-sided fountain at its base. It came from the Temple of the Sun in Heliopolis, near Cairo, where it had been placed by Ramses II. Augustus brought it to Rome to grace a temple to Apollo at the Circus Maximus. It was moved to its present location in 1589. It was referred to as a "fiery column," because it is made of red granite. Four lions at its base were added in 1823.

Piazza Montecitorio, behind Piazza Colonna
This obelisk with hieroglyphics first stood in Heliopolis. It was placed in the Campus Martius by Augustus. Rediscovered in fragments near the Church of San Lorenzo in the early 16th century, it wasn't raised until 1792, at which time it was moved to its present location.

Villa Mattei (Celimontana), *Piazza della Navicella*
This obelisk is said to stand on top of the severed hand of a workman, who didn't move out of the way quickly enough when it was put in place. Only its top portion is Egyptian; the rest is Roman.

Santa Maria Maggiore, *Piazza dell'Esquilino*
Piazza del Quirinale
These two obelisks were originally brought from Egypt by Claudius in A.D. 57 and stood at the entrance of the mausoleum of Augustus. Santa Maria Maggiore's was moved by Sixtus V, and the Quirinale's by Pius VI.

Trinità de' Monti, *Spanish Steps*
This Roman obelisk once stood in the gardens of the Palace of Sallust, between Via Veneto and the Borghese Gardens. It was moved to the top of the Spanish Steps in 1789.

Garden of the Pincio
The Roman obelisk at the crossroads in the Garden of the Pincio was erected (as described in its hieroglyphics) by Hadrian (right) and was dedicated to his slave and lover, Antinous (background), who may have accidentally drowned in the Nile in A.D. 131. Hadrian's wife, Sabina (left), may have had him killed.

This Egyptian obelisk without hieroglyphics, from Heliopolis, was originally in Caligula's private circus on the Vatican Hill. It was erected in the center of the piazza in 1586.

Fontana dei Quattro Fiumi, *Piazza Navona*

The figures representing the four rivers of Gianlorenzo Bernini's fountain cluster around this Roman obelisk, which formerly stood in the Circus of Maxentius on the Appian Way.

Piazza Minerva

A small sixth-century-B.C. Egyptian obelisk is now carried on the back of an elephant—also known as *il pulcino,* the kid—in the piazza in front of Chiesa Santa Maria sopra Minerva, the ancient site of Roman temples to Isis and Minerva. The obelisk, which is inscribed with a few lines of hieroglyphics, stood in front of the Temple of Isis and was moved by Pope Alexander VII in 1667. The elephant was carved in the same year by Ercole Ferrata but was designed by Bernini.

Santa Maria sopra Minerva, built in 1284, is Rome's only truly Gothic church. It contains the tomb of scholar-turned-cardinal Pietro Bembo, who is more closely associated with Venice than with Rome. Most of the remains of Santa Caterina di Siena are here as well.

Piazza della Rotonda

The fountain in the center of the piazza in front of the Pantheon holds the top part of a broken obelisk, originally from Heliopolis. It first stood at the nearby Temple of Isis, close to what is now Santa Maria sopra Minerva. It was moved in 1711 by Pope Clement XI.

The Augusteum

Between Via Ripetta and the Corso

This mausoleum was built to house the remains of Augustus Caesar.[1] It also holds the bodies of his grandson, Marcellus; son-in-law, Agrippa; sister, Octavia; and wife, Livia. Also interred are Tiberius, Caligula, and the little-known emperor Nerva, among others. Claudius is here as well, without his wife, Messalina.

1 Augustus died in A.D. 14. His funeral pyre burned for five days.

THE PINCIO

The Pincio, the eighth of Rome's seven hills, is covered with extensive gardens. Although lovely to stroll through now, these gardens have a tragic history. They were part of the villa of Lucullus (above), a wealthy general in the first century B.C. (The adjective *Lucullan,* meaning lavish, comes from his reputation as a host of splendid feasts.) The villa changed hands several times and came to be owned by the unfortunate Valerius Asiaticus, who killed himself rather than relinquish the villa to the covetous Messalina (below), the fifth wife of Emperor Claudius. Her greed, along with her disgraceful orgies and lies, led to condemnation by Claudius after she divorced him, then sneakily remarried. She was urged by her family to honorably take her own life. Too cowardly to do so, she was run through with a sword by one of the soldiers who brought the order for her execution.

Nero was later buried on the Pincio, and rumors that his ghost stalked the hill began to circulate. A walnut tree, which supposedly grew from his grave, attracted demonic crows.

CAPUCHIN CATACOMBS

When the bell tolled for one of the saintly *cappuccini,* Capuchin monks, of Santa Maria della Concezione, room was made to bury him—in holy soil brought especially from Jerusalem—by ousting a previous tenant. This tradition lasted from 1528 until 1870. Like writer Nathaniel Hawthorne, who wrote of the Capuchins in *The Marble Faun* in 1860, you, too, can see these disinterred remains in the semi-subterranean crypt. In a series of four chapels, the scapulae, clavicles, and vertebrae of some 4,000 evictees have been arranged into crosses, hearts, and crowns. Some are complete: wisps of tendons and cartilage hold together limbs and torsos and skulls and jaws, mostly hidden under decaying hooded brown robes.

Take time to see the church itself. In the first chapel is a painting (1630) by Bolognese artist Guido Reni, showing the Archangel Michael trampling the Devil.

Santa Maria della Concezione (dei Cappuccini)
Via Vittorio Veneto 27

In Hawthorne's *Marble Faun,* Donatello, the character who resembles the Faun of Praxiteles (background), pushes a man off the Tarpeian Rock. The next day he and his American friend Miriam go to the Capuchin church and, by coincidence, see the body of the same man, a monk, laid out on a bier. Hawthorne describes the corpse's half-closed eyes seemingly watching the couple as they stare at him in the flickering candlelight, while a ghastly chant comes from the crypt below.

As patron saint of musicians and composers, St Cecilia is serenaded every 21 and 22 November.

SANTA CECILIA

This church is named after the aristocratic Cecilia, who was condemned to be executed in A.D. 230, after converting a number of people, including her husband, Valerian, to Christianity. First, she was put into her own baths, which were heated to extreme temperatures. However, a cooling rain shower miraculously doused the fires. A beheading was attempted, but the executioner was unable, after three tries, to sever her head. Gravely injured, Cecilia continued to preach for the next three days, but then died.

Pope Urban had her interred in the catacombs of St Calixtus. In 821, her burial place was divulged in a vision to Paschal I, who transferred her to this church (rebuilt in 1725), which was constructed upon the foundations of a church that stood on what was left of her house. Her sarcophagus was opened in 1599, reputedly giving sculptor Stefano Maderno a chance to copy her pose for his *Figure of the Martyred St Cecilia* (above), a sculpture for which the church is justly famous.

SANTO BAMBINO

The bejeweled, chubby Christ child, Santo Bambino, attends Mass every Christmas Day at the high altar of Santa Maria d'Aracœli, then returns for the rest of the year to his crib in the Sacristy, when he's not attending the sick, to whom he is taken by taxi.

The Santissimo Bambino, originally carved from cedar by a monk, was left on the beds of the sick until a miracle cure was effected.[2] The practice changed in the 19th century when a woman, covetous of the powerful doll, slyly re-created him right down to the smallest detail. She then feigned illness and had the real Bambino brought to her. She stripped him of his gold and silver clothes and put them on her replica, which she returned to the church. That night the monks were awakened by a terrible pealing of bells and a frantic knocking at the west door, under which a tiny pair of bare feet could be seen. Hastily opening the door, they found the naked and shivering Bambino trying to get back in. From then on, the monks didn't let him out of their sight. Unfortunately, in 1994, Bambinello was stolen again; an olive-wood replacement stands in for him now.

2 Charles Dickens saw the Bambino in 1844 and figured that the shock of seeing the inert baby lying on the bed would kill rather than cure.

Santa Maria d'Aracœli
Off Piazza del Campidoglio

Monks used to pull teeth for free every morning on the stairs linking Santa Maria d'Aracœli to the Palazzo Senatorio.

Santo Bambino, also known as Bambinello and il Santissimo Bambino.

San Giovanni Decollato
*Via di San Giovanni
Decollato*

St John the Baptist,
*detail, by Leonardo da
Vinci.*

San Silvestro in Capite
Piazza San Silvestro

Palazzo Doria Pamphili
*Piazza del Collegio
Romano*

Palazzo dei Conservatori
Musei Capitolini
Piazza del Campidoglio

THE BEHEADED ST JOHN

On a search for the headless St John the
Baptist, one could do worse than to visit San
Giovanni Decollato in Trastevere. This was
where the Confraternità della Misericordia di
San Giovanni Decollato (founded in 1488)
devoted themselves to caring for criminals condemned, like St John, to lose their heads.

Charles Dickens, a witness to a beheading
ministered to by the Confraternità, convinced
himself that the sight would be instructive. He
joined a relatively large crowd of housewives,
soldiers, children, and pastry cooks, watched
the execution, and went away much sobered.

In Dickens's time, the approach to the church
was lined with heads of the saint, carved into
the stone above the doors of the houses. Inside
the church, by appointment only, you can still
see Vasari's *Beheading of St John* (1553).

Extant St John relics throughout Italy
include many heads and enough bones to re-
create several saints. In Rome, San Silvestro in
Capite claims to have the saint's actual head.

For artwork around Rome, visit the beheading in Titian's *Salomé* (1516) at the Palazzo
Doria Pamphili. Caravaggio's *St John the Baptist*
(1595–96), of the living apostle, is at the Palazzo
dei Conservatori.

THE LAOCOÖN

Possibly the most celebrated statue
in Rome is the group known as the
Laocoön (detail, right), showing the death
of Laocoön, a priest of Apollo. When it
was unearthed from Nero's Domus
Aurelius, Golden House, in 1506, it was
missing an arm; an ungainly replacement
was fitted on and stayed there until the
real arm was found in 1905, tucked away
in a stonemason's studio. The statue,
along with the equally famous Apollo
Belvedere (below, right), was temporarily
taken to the Louvre by Napoleon. Both
are now housed in the Vatican Museum's
Museo Pio-Clementino.

In 1839, travel guide writer Mariana
Starke advised visiting the Vatican museums by
torch-light, "as the torch, like Promethean fire,
makes every statue live; in consequence of
which, perhaps, the most stupendous efforts of
the Grecian chisel were originally placed in
subterranean baths."

She reckoned that four three-pound wax
torches would be adequate to light the statues
and reminded travelers to seek advance permission for their evening visit from the pope's
maggiordomo.

Museo Pio-Clementino,
Musei del Vaticano
San Pietro,
Belvedere Pavilion,
Vatican

Michelangiolesco: grand, in the manner of Michelangelo

San Pietro in Vincoli
Piazza di San Pietro in Vincoli

MICHELANGELO

The output of painter, sculptor, architect, and poet Michelangelo was prodigious. In addition to his creations for Lorenzo de' Medici in Florence, he sculpted *Moses* (San Pietro in Vincoli) and the *Pietà* (St Peter's) and painted the fresco *The Last Judgment* (Sistine Chapel, St Peter's) for Pope Julius II in Rome.

The figures in his *Last Judgment* were controversial because of their nudity. Daniele da Volterra was commissioned to paint trousers on them and subsequently became known as *il Braghettone,* the breeches maker. Michelangelo has also been connected with clothing: the Vatican's Swiss guards wear a distinctively striped uniform (left), said to have been created by him.

He designed the dome of St Peter's (background), after envying Brunelleschi's in Florence, and reputedly positioned his tomb at Santa Croce in order to get the best view of that dome, should the doors be open.

Michelangelo died in Rome but wished to be buried in Florence. To keep Romans from stealing him, his casket was spirited away to Florence, disguised as merchandise.

GIANLORENZO BERNINI

For sheer physicality, nothing can beat the work of precocious sculptor Gianlorenzo Bernini, he of the "well-twirled moustache." This miracle worker in marble started his sculpting career in his early teens. A pious and passionate man known for large gestures and emotions, he was also an architect, painter, theatrical producer, and composer. He worked for eight popes, made Rome a gallery for his art, and was duly loathed by John Ruskin, an outspoken critic of the Baroque. If a statue has excessive but beautiful drapery, you can be pretty sure it's a Bernini. Even his Scala Regia in the Vatican looks like tumbling cloth. To judge Bernini for yourself, take the following tour (don't forget the colonnaded piazza outside St Peter's, as well as the baldachin and many tombs inside).

Ecstasy of St Teresa (1646): Set in center stage at Santa Maria della Vittoria, watched over by a marble audience, and guarded by an ambiguously smiling angel, the Spanish saint, Teresa of Avila, floats on a cloud, stunningly oblivious to all in her swoon. *Baedeker's* called it "notorious [though] masterly, whatever may be thought of the spirit."

The Death of the Blessed Ludovica Albertoni (1674): Forget about St Francis of Assisi's stone pillow here at San Francesco a Ripa; instead,

"Holy Bernini!"—
Wilhelmine Buchholz,
1889

Dickens declared that Baroque was the work of "breezy maniacs ... whose smallest vein, or artery, is as big as an ordinary forefinger; whose hair is like a nest of lively snakes; and whose attitudes put all other extravagance to shame."

Santa Maria della Vittoria
Cappella Cornaro
Via XX Settembre 17
Via Veneto

San Francesco a Ripa
Cappella Altieri
Piazza San Francesco
d'Assisi

spend time in the Altieri chapel, gaping at Bernini's marvel of drapery, the intensely pious 17th-century Ludovica Albertoni, and try not to think about the fact that she is portrayed in her death throes.

The Bernini Rooms
Museo e Galleria
Borghese
Piazzale Scipione,
Borghese Gardens

Pluto and Persephone (1622): Pluto's stony fingers leave heartbreaking impressions on Persephone's Carrara marble thigh, and the tears trickling down her cheek add to the emotion of this seductive statue. Other Bernini statues at the Borghese include *David, Ænus carrying Anchises,* and *Apollo and Daphne* (opposite).

Santa Bibiana
Via Giovanni Giolitti
154

Santa Bibiana (1626): Bernini designed this church in which his statue of Santa Bibiana, who watches over those who are hungover, displays the leather cords (they look like palm fronds) with which she was whipped. She was martyred for her beliefs around A.D. 360.

Fontana dei Quattro Fiumi
Fontana del Moro
Piazza Navona

Fountain of the Four Rivers (1651; background): This fountain features allegorical figures of the Ganges, Danube, Plata, and Nile. (Nile is said to be holding up his hand to shield his view of Borromini's overwrought facade on the Church of Sant'Agnese, facing him.)[3] Bernini also created the *Fountain of the Moor* found in the same piazza.

3 Sant'Agnese was exposed naked in A.D. 304 at a brothel on the site of the current church, to force her to renounce her faith. She's shown covering herself with her hair, which miraculously grew to protect her modesty.

Sant'Ivo alla Sapienza
Corso del Rinascimento 40, near Piazza Navona

San Carlo alle Quattro Fontane
Via del Quirinale 23

Palazzo Pamphili
Piazza Navona

FRANCESCO BORROMINI

Borromini was a controversial but influential architect who created dazzling geometric forms that flew in the face of tradition. His spiral dome of Sant'Ivo (background) and the ovoid dome of San Carlo are examples of his genius for use of limited space.

Borromini and Bernini worked together on a number of projects, but at the death of Bernini's patron, Pope Urban VIII, Borromini declared Bernini to be incompetent. As a result, part of Bernini's work at St Peter's was destroyed and his commissions from the new pope, Innocent X, halted. Borromini profited from Bernini's fall by securing a commission for the pope's own palace, the Palazzo Pamphili, and the adjacent church, Sant'Agnese.

Tormented with melancholy, Borromini committed suicide in 1667, the year that San Carlo was completed.

> Borromini being mad, I am surprised at nothing that he has done. I am surprised only that, after having built one church, he was ever employed on a second: yet the man went on, murdering the most sumptuous edifices in Rome, until at last he murdered himself.—Joseph Forsyth, 1803

A Famous Visitor
JOHANN JOACHIM WINCKELMANN: 1717–68

*W*inckelmann, a Prussian art expert, lived in Italy from 1755 until his death, and his writings on art, including his *Geschichte der Kunst des Alterhums, History of Ancient Art,* were much appreciated by Grand Tourists such as Goethe. He converted to Catholicism when he was told that was to be the price for the post of librarian for Cardinal Archinto. Then, with Cardinal Alessandro Albani as his patron, he became Director of Antiquities, responsible for the care and documentation of Rome's monuments and art. He made his home at Albani's sumptuous villa, east of the Borghese Gardens. His studies of antiquities also took him to Florence and Naples.

Cardinal Albani, a renowned art collector, lost 294 statues to Napoleon. They were restored to him in 1814, but he sold them in Paris rather than pay their transport back.

Galleria Albani e Collezione Archeologica, Villa Albani
Via di Villa Albani
(by appointment only)

Winckelmann was one of Italy's most knowledgeable and farsighted art historians, but that didn't stopp rumors from circulating about his private life. He was apparently eccentric, with a penchant for young boys, including castrati, and is said to have tested his homosexuality by lying naked with Margaret Mengs, the wife of his friend, Bohemian neoclassical painter Anton Raphael (Ralph) Mengs. His irregular life led him to make at least one very unfortunate friendship. Returning from a visit to Vienna, where he was feted by Empress Maria Theresa, he was murdered in his Trieste hotel room by Francesco Arcangeli, an 18-year-old scullery boy, who, it is said, was out to rob Winckelmann of some gold medals he had shown him. Arcangeli shortly after was executed for his crime.

A Famous Visitor
EDWARD GIBBON: 1737–94

In 1764, Edward Gibbon, the 27-year-old future author of *Decline and Fall of the Roman Empire,* left England for a visit to Italy. He made the usual stops on the Grand Tour, but was so taken at being in Rome that he wrote, "Several days of intoxication were lost or enjoyed before I could descend to a cool and minute investigation." He decided to record the empire's demise while at the Forum one moonlit night, soaking up the atmosphere and listening to barefoot monks singing vespers.

The first volume of his monumental work didn't appear until 1776; the complete opus was finished in 1787. The first edition sold out in days. Readers were drawn to his frank and humorous descriptions of an amoral age. Although he rendered the licentious parts in Latin only— or as he put it, "in the decent obscurity of a learned language"—critics vilified him for his indecorous language. He was also seen to be wanting of Christian sentiment. Having been won over to the glories of the Roman Republic, he determined that Christianity had led to its downfall and, for that, needed to be chastised.

Many historical details found in *Decline and Fall* have since been corrected or modified, and the writing is now seen to be occasionally tortured, even obtuse. Nevertheless, Gibbon's work is still considered a striking example of the deep knowledge of a brilliant and eclectic mind.

A Notable Visitor
MARIE-PAULINE BONAPARTE, PRINCESS BORGHESE: 1780–1825

𝒫auline, one of Napoleon's sisters,[4] lived a whirlwind life, especially once she married Prince Camillo Borghese in 1802. She posed nude for Canova in 1805;[5] the resulting statue, *Venus,* is on display at the Museo e Galleria Borghese. When asked if it wasn't difficult to take off her clothes to pose for the artist, she replied that his studio was well heated. Her husband had a problem with the statue, though, and locked it up. His distaste for it may not have been from prudery, but may have

Santa Maria Maggiore
Piazza di Santa Maria Maggiore

had more to do with his decision to break his connection with the Bonapartes after Napoleon's fall in 1814. He and Pauline separated around this time, and Pauline lived briefly with her brother on Elba.

Pauline died in Florence, but now lies in an unmarked tomb in Santa Maria Maggiore.

---

4 Napoleon's other sisters were also well placed in Italy: Caroline-Marie Annonciade was queen of Naples from 1808 until 1814, and Marie-Anne-Elisa became Grand-Duchess of Tuscany from 1809 until 1814.

5 Canova presumably got a chance to see Napoleon with his pants down, as he sculpted him in the nude, too.

Boswell, best known as the author of *The Life of Samuel Johnson*, toured the Continent in 1765–66, resolutely ignoring his father's demands that he come back home to practice law. Boswell took advantage of his tour to meet Voltaire and Rousseau. He also befriended Pasquale Paoli, a heroic Corsican patriot, and promoted Corsica's fight for independence. While in Italy, Boswell preferred to be called Giacomo.

BOSWELL'S VENEREAL TOUR

Here's a distraction: a detour following James Boswell's famous Venereal Tour of 1765. Literarily, that is, not literally.

Because most Englishmen went to Italy with the idea that "a really complete tour included at least one Italian countess," Boswell, a Scot, thought that meant at least one countess in every town. When he couldn't get a countess, he settled for a respectable married lady, and when he couldn't get one of those, he slept with just about any woman. Boswell explained his behavior this way: "It was the custom of the society in which I lived. I yielded to custom."

This is Boswell's Tour in a nutshell: Turin: one countess, two ladies, a "pretty girl"; Rome: a "girl every day"; Naples: a singer, more "willing girls"; Rome again: "prostitutes licensed by the Cardinal Vicar," "willing girls," a Florentine lady, VD and body lice; Venice: a lady, a "pretty dancer," "willing girls," and VD again; Florence: "willing girls" and VD again; Siena: two ladies.

Boswell's experiences were far from uncommon. Nor was he the only visitor to Italy to contract syphilis. Stendhal, whose affairs were outdone only by Boswell and Byron, probably picked up syphilis in Milan in 1800. It plagued him throughout his life. As for Boswell, his enduring desire for female charms kept him seeking cures long after his Italian sojourn.

ROMAN CAFFÈ AND GRAND TOURISTS

Visitors who seek hints of Rome's vanished past
will certainly want to visit the former site of the
Caffè degli Inglesi. It was once a favorite haunt
of artists and Grand Tourists attracted by its central location and exotic decor: Egyptian-style
murals, painted in the 1760s by Giovanni Battista
Piranesi. The pyramids, obelisks, hieroglyphics,
and sphinxes now exist only in Piranesi's book
*Diverse maniere d'adornare . . . dall'architettura
egizia, etrusca e greca.* Prints from this book are
found in Rome's many bookstores.

Piranesi studied architecture and stage
design and became a draftsman to the papal
court, then opened a print shop on Rome's
Corso. His books *Le antichità romane* and
Carceri, Prisons, with illustrations of fantastic
buildings based on ancient structures, provoked
Horace Walpole to write, "He has imagined
scenes that would startle geometry."

For an antique *caffè* experience, go to the
Greco, established in 1760, and drink coffee
with the ghosts of Goethe and Casanova. Hans
Christian Andersen liked this place so much
that he lived in the same building. Another
long-established *caffè* is the Pace, established in
1800, with decor dating from 1900.

Caffè degli Inglesi
*Via Due Macelli and
Piazza di Spagna*
Used by James
Boswell as his mailing
address in 1765.

Caffè Greco
Via Condotti 86
On 24 March 1824,
Leo XII, wishing to
discourage the dissi-
dents that patronized
the Greco, declared
that any citizen going
into the *caffè* would
be thrown in prison
for three months. The
owner retaliated by
serving customers
through a window.

Antico Caffè della Pace
*Via della Pace 5, near
Piazza Navona*

Cimitero Protestante (aka
Acattolico or degli Inglesi)
Via Caio Cestio 6
Testaccio

"We have been burn-
ing the bodies of
Shelley and Williams
on the seashore . . .
You can have no idea
what an extraordinary
effect such a funeral
pile has, on a desolate
shore, with mountains
in the back-ground
and the sea before,
and the singular
appearance the salt
and frankincense gave
to the flame. All of
Shelley was con-
sumed, except his
heart, which would
not take the flame,
and is now preserved
in spirits of wine."
—Byron, 1822

ROME'S PROTESTANT CEMETERY

Non-Catholic burials were barely
tolerated in 19th-century Rome. They
had to be conducted at night, the graves could
not bear crosses, and inscriptions had to be pre-
approved. Nonetheless, the Protestant Cemetery
became a popular resting ground for foreigners,
including American sculptor William Wetmore
Story; English historian John Addington
Symonds; Edward John Trelawney, adventurer
and friend of Shelley and Byron; Joseph Severn,
Keats's faithful friend and British Consul at
Rome; and Constance Fenimore Woolson,
American writer and companion of Henry
James, who flung herself out a window in Venice.

The most famous grave belongs to English
poet Percy Bysshe Shelley, a victim, along with
his friend Edward Williams, of a boating acci-
dent in July 1822, near Viareggio. Some sources
say his grave contains his heart, the only part
that didn't burn when he was cremated by
Trelawney, Byron, and English writer Leigh
Hunt on the beach where his body washed up.
Other sources claim the heart was plucked out
of the fire by Trelawney. Hunt wanted it des-
perately, but they decided that Mary Shelley
should have it. When she died, it was reputedly
found—desiccated and shrunken—in her copy
of her husband's *Adonais.* It may have been lost
at that point or added to Shelley's grave.

IL CONGRESSO DEGLI ARGUTI

Rome has six statues known as the Congress of Shrewds, so called because of the many satirical notes that have been affixed to and written on them since the early 16th century. The most famous, Pasquino, is found on the northwest corner of Piazza di Pasquino. Most of his features have been obliterated by time, weather, and the pasted-on messages, which came to be known as *pasquils* or *pasquinades,* named so, according to one account, after a shoemaker or tailor notorious for his scribbled lampoons. This outspoken critic of authority, who had the statue "speak" for him, relied on the safety of anonymity, as free speech was at that time actively and most cruelly discouraged.[6] Pasquino was also considered the first publishing house for 16th-century blackmailer Pietro Aretino. As his writings were bitter, satiric, and indecent, he couldn't have found a better spot to launch his career or sharpen his wits.

Pope Hadrian VI contemplated the benefits of having Pasquino tossed into the Tiber but backed down when he considered the scorn he'd receive for punishing a block of stone.

Rebuttals to Pasquino's comments were attached to Marforio, a statue of a river god,

Pasquino
Piazza di Pasquino,
west of Piazza Navona

Madama Lucrezia
Palazzetto Venezia,
near San Marco

L'Abate Luigi
Piazza Vidoni,
off Corso V Emanuele,
near Sant'Andrea della
Valle

Il Facchino
Fontanella del Facchino
Via Lata

Marforio
Piazza del Campidoglio

Il Babuino
Via del Babuino,
off Piazza di Spagna

Babbuino: baboon; silly, ridiculous person

6 Pasquino's messages today—often Socialist propaganda— show a grinding sincerity and a marked lack of humor.

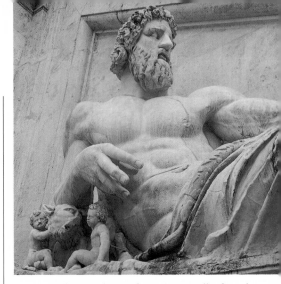

"We inkpot users have a terrible lot of work to do to lift up into the sky names which are weighed to earth with the lead of every kind of lack of worth."—Pietro Aretino, on "those who buy fame."

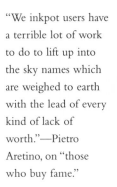

once on the Via di Marforio (originally found in the Forum of Mars, above). He shot his mouth off too often and now resides in the Piazza del Campidoglio, the spacious and elegant square designed by Michelangelo.

The other four talking statues include the only talking woman, Madama Lucrezia (a priestess of Isis), now lacking much of her face through erosion. L'Abate (Abbot) Luigi was formerly a statue of a now-unidentifiable emperor; the present-day head was taken from another statue. Il Babuino (the baboon) is located in what was previously the foreigners' quarter, a safer place to leave incendiary messages and lampoons. Il Facchino (the porter) is the only non-Roman statue of the bunch; he's part of a fountain and is shown with a cask, out of which pours water.

SOUNDING GOOD ALLA ROMANA

Rome, like Milan, is a city focused on style. But *fare una bella figura,* to look good, you need more than to be *acchittato,* dressed up with particular elegance. You need the right attitude. Here are some words to help you with your pose:

Borghese: person of the middle class
Cose all'italiana: all things Italian
Furbo(a): smart ass; *fesso(a):* dimwit. *Furbi* look down on *fessi.* The roles change randomly and quickly.
Fresco: brazen, shameless
Gregorio: the behind
Mammismo: mother love
Mozzarella: spineless man

The following will help those who want to complain or try to get something done:

Aduggiarsi: *Non aduggiarmi con le tue lamentele,* don't bug me with your complaints.
Albergo (lit. hotel): police headquarters
E allora?: so what?
Così vanno le cose: that's the way it goes.
Disinvoltura: casualness, ease, indifference
Fregare: to rub, cheat; *me ne frego,* I don't care; *chi se ne frega?,* who gives a damn?; *menefreghisti:* those who don't care; *menefreghismo:* the "don't care" attitude.
Pizzardone: Roman policeman

Vocabolario Romano

Another conversational focus in Rome is getting ahead. Here are some words to help you do just that:

Arrangiarsi: to find a way around something
Grattagratta (lit. scratch-scratch): greedy politician
Portoghese: gate-crasher
Raccomandazione: personal recommendation; *raccomandatario:* the recommended one
Vada a nome mio: tell them I sent you

Excursion from Rome: Lago di Bolsena

The deep waters of volcanic Lake Bolsena, north of Rome, are home to *anguille,* eels, a delicacy cherished since Etruscan times. But few have taken their fondness for them as far as French Pope Martin IV, otherwise known as Simon de Brie. Disparagingly referred to as he of "the most puckered face," Martin died Easter morning, 1285, from cramming himself too heartily with eels.[7] He was buried in the Duomo at Perugia and, for his greed, Dante wrote him off as a glutton and dropped him into purgatory (Canto 24). The citizens of Bolsena still send the pope a case of eels each Christmas.

According to Bolognese Jacopo della Lana, a 14th-century commentator on Dante's *Divine Comedy* who wouldn't pull the wool over his reader's eyes, eels such as those served to Pope Martin were first lovingly suffocated in Vernaccia wine,[8] then were stuffed with cheese, eggs, and spices and roasted.

Restaurants in the town of Bolsena and around the lake serve eel steaks grilled with pepper, wine, and bay leaves.

"Gaudent anguillae
Quia mortuus hic
*   jacet ille*
Qui quasi morte reas
Excoriabat eas."

"There was joy
   among the eels
When death laid him
   by the heels
For he skinned 'em
   and sorted 'em
As though death had
   county-courted
   'em."

—Epitaph written
around the time of
Pope Martin IV's death

7 At least these eels were raised *allo stato naturale,* naturally; Pollio, one of antiquity's vile personalities, fed his eels with slaves.

8 Pliny suggested serving eels putrified in wine (vintage unimportant) to cure alcoholics.

الدكتور

TABACCHI
LAVORATI

VOX
CLUB

proiet

d...
ses oeu...
...he ad...   admire...
...gs f...which   quels ell...
...rks clearly re-   L'on re...
...ta Tiepolo is   nelle in...na...
...extra   chromat...
...f colour   les plus...

...o (Ven...
...lebre u...
XVIII. Su...
...mes sobre t...
constituyen...
...scin...a...

NAPOLI WARNING
1:20.000   ...CT POWER BEFO...
Metri   LIGHTS AND A...
                ...CAL COMPONEN...

CAL 99

品恐ッ...
...付の最大の特徴て

la car...ente s...

1862

Napoli

IF THE RESPONSE of most non-Italian speakers to Naples could be said in one word, it would be the unintentional but appropriate mangling of the name of the noisy, grimy district in the city's heart, *Spaccanapoli,* split Naples, into *Scappanapoli,* flee Naples.

What could be better, given that almost every newly arriving northerner will be scarppering to nearby Sorrento without so much as a shiver at the grand *memento mori* that is Naples. For this is a city where death is proclaimed at every corner: from hushed churches with their skulls, ex-votos, and relics; from shrines filled with flickering candlelight, fading roses, and weeping Madonnas; and from catacombs and cemeteries with their unabashed displays of remains.

Spaccanapoli is a labyrinth adorned with hues of dust and decay that draws you in and holds you. There is a new sight around every corner. Much is explosive: a kid bursts out of an alley on a motorbike three times his size; traders shout frantically at the rag market; an age-old argument erupts between neighbors.

Junk shops, grocers, churches, and stalls selling *pizza al taglio,* pizza by

Napoletanamente: in the Neapolitan way

Napoletanismo: Naples-style talk

Napoletana: a coffee pot; a hand in the card game *tresette*

Mezzogiorno: South Italy; also midday

Mezzoguanto: fingerless glove

"Naples begins nowhere and finishes also nowhere."
—Wilhelmine Buchholz, 1887

"Our eagerness to see sights has been repressed at Naples only by finding everything a sight."—Hester Piozzi, 1785

BACKGROUND: *Naples, 1885.*

the slice, abound. The aroma of pizza grapples with the fragrance of fresh *sfogliatella,* flaky pastry filled with sweet ricotta, which in turn battles with the odors of coffee, exhaust, ripe vegetables, life. Crumbling walls are the canvas for an infinite layering of posters, from advertisements for a play to pious proclamations of upcoming saints' days. Newspapers, fruit peels, and broken record albums pile up on the pavement, a treasure trove for the archaeologically inclined visitor.

Along streets with such names as Santa Maria di Constantinopoli and San Bagio dei Librai are antiquarian bookstores, their shelves jammed with thousands of books on Naples. Can so much truly have been written about one place alone?

Naples beckons you to scratch through its surfaces and to immerse yourself in its core. Its monuments and museums are more than just edifices; they are also the streets and stalls ripe with life, lived and living. Don't you love this city already?

"[In Naples] a man known to be poor is scarcely considered a man at all, and if a man is believed to be rich, his life is in danger. From this it follows that in such places, as is the practice, one should keep his financial status a mystery so that the public does not know whether to despise you or murder you. And you then can be what men ordinarily are, half-despised and half-respected, sometimes threatened, sometimes safe."
—Giacomo Leopardi, c. 1837

Mercati
Pignasecca
near Piazza Carità

Sant'Antonio
Via Sant'Antonio Abate

Porta Nolana
Via Carmignano

Torretta
Viale Gramsci

Cimitero Monumentale
Via Nuova Poggioreale

PHOTOGRAPHY PROHIBITED

What could be more typical than a tourist taking a photo of a lively Mediterranean fruit and vegetable market? In Naples, if the police had their way, no shutters would click, because these *mercati,* markets, are run by the snapshot-sensitive Camòrra (from Spanish for quarrel), Naples's equivalent to Sicily's Mafia. The police don't want to pick up any more wounded tourists than necessary.

Photography is also energetically discouraged at Naples's Cimitero Monumentale, though the reason for this ban isn't clear. A great deal of discretion is needed here, as it is difficult to suppress the temptation to photograph the tombs built as Egyptian temples, Palladian villas, Art Deco houses, and Bedouin tents.

STREET LINGO

Neapolitan slang includes several essential words for tip: *buonamano, mancia, da bere, bottiglia, caffè,* and *fumata.* The *facchino,* porter, is still a common sight; less so the *lazzarone,* a laze about, heel, or cad. A *scippatore,* bag snatcher, is a constant worry, and the *scugnizzi,* street urchins, are ubiquitous. *Sbirri,* police spies or police, can be found around Italy, but are especially prevalent here.

SPAGHETTI BELLISSIMI

There are no *camerieri,* waiters, in Naples more swaggering than the well-fed bunch at the Bellini, who bounce off one another as they rush between tightly packed tables laden with plates of pizzas, pastas, and seafood. Note that the last is, as is usual, at *prezzo da vedere,* price to be seen, not for the faint of heart. Ask first, if you're on a budget.

Their pasta with seafood in parchment is exquisite. It's doubtful they'd divulge their secret, but try the following substitute. It feeds four as a *primo,* appetizer, or two as a *secondo,* main course.

Preheat oven to 200°C/400°F. Cook 150 g/ ⅓ lb. pasta in boiling, salted water; drain and rinse. Sauté, in olive oil and white wine, 12 peeled prawns and 150 g/⅓ lb. cleaned, sliced squid.[1] Season with salt and pepper. Chop up 15 to 20 cherry tomatoes and lots of fresh basil. Place equal portions of seafood, pasta, tomatoes, and basil onto 2 or 4 sheets of parchment paper. Add oregano, salt, pepper, and olive oil to taste. Fold the parchment around the ingredients, set on a rack inside a baking pan, fill with boiling water to just below the rack, and cook for 15 minutes. Open the packets, and garnish with fresh basil.

1 Try any combination of seafood: clams, mussels, and white-fleshed fish such as sole or snapper. Shellfish should be fully cooked before adding to the pasta.

Ristorante Bellini
Piazza Bellini

Augustus Hare's bad pizza day, c. 1883: "The horrible condiment called *pizza* (made of dough baked with garlic, rancid bacon, and strong cheese) is esteemed a feast."

Aglio: garlic
Mangiar l'aglio: to eat garlic; also to rage in silence

Cappella di Sansevero

Via Francesco de
Sanctis 19

AN ALCHEMICAL CHAPEL

This extravagant 18th-century chapel and
sepulchre is tucked away on a dead end off
Vico San Domenico Maggiore. It was built
by the alchemist and inventor Raimondo di
Sangro, Prince of Sansevero and a Grand Master
of the Masons, whose name shares its root with
sangue, blood, an appropriate link as he is said
to have found a formula for artificial blood. In

the crypt stand two anatomical
specimens, examples of his cadaverous experiments, for which he
was excommunicated.

The chapel contains some
splendid marble statues, often
mistakenly attributed to the
Baroque genius Bernini. They
include *Il disinganno,* variously
translated as *Deception,*
Disenchantment, Despair, or
Deluded Vice (left); *Modesty*, a
voluptuously, yet carefully veiled
female figure by Antonio
Corradini; and the inexplicably
moving, recumbent *Veiled Christ*
by Giuseppe Sanmartino. This
last figure was carved from one
block of marble; the veil is a
marvel of translucence.

A MODERN-DAY SAINT

The Gesù Nuovo chapels dedicated to St
Giuseppe Moscati, the Neapolitan doctor
canonized in 1987, only hint at the veneration
in which he is held. Moscati died in 1927 at
the age of 47, ostensibly from a life of exhaust-
ing work, looking after the city's sick and poor.
His death was mourned by all who knew him,
especially those who had benefited from his
attention. Soon after he died, miraculous cures
were reported, including a recovery from
Addison's disease and another from leukemia,
both, it was claimed, effected by his spirit. The
Vatican found the claims well grounded and
declared him a saint.

Testimonials from hundreds of people, in
the form of letters and ex-votos, cover the
walls of one chapel. A large illuminated photograph of Moscati watches over another chapel.
Also displayed is a re-creation of his study from
the Ospedale degli Incurabili.

The pharmacy of this hospital was never
modernized and long maintained the appearance of a traditional apothecary shop. Its pol-
ished wood shelves were stacked to the frescoed
ceiling with majolica jars, with such labels as
"Belladonnae" and "Quininae Sulphas." It was
once open to the public, but a recent attempt to
visit there was met with the information that it
had become dilapidated and dangerous to enter.

Chiesa Gesù Nuovo
Piazza del Gesù Nuovo

Ospedale degli Incurabili
Farmacia
Via Armanni

The Duomo

The Duomo is one of some 200 churches[2] in the city. Pilgrims flock here because of St Januarius, the fifth-century Bishop of Benevento, who came to Naples with six assistants to help Christians. His mission was crushed when he was captured, taken to Pozzuoli, and left in the amphitheater at the mercy of wild beasts. When those beasts turned up their noses at the offering, he was thrown into a furnace but didn't burn. Beheading finished him off.

Two bottles of his blood were saved and taken to Naples. When the dried-out blood was found to liquefy on certain dates, seekers of solace crowded into the church to pray to the saint. Ever since, on 19 September, 16 December, and the first Saturday in May, old and young take their places in the church and plead with the saint until the blood liquefies.

Visitor Michael Kelly witnessed the miracle of liquifaction in 1779:

> "Pray use your influence with St Gennaro! Pray induce him to work the miracle! Do we not love him? Do we not worship him?" But when they found the Saint inexorable, they changed their note, and seemed resolved to abuse him into compliance. They all at once cried out, "Porco di

Chiesa di San Gennaro
Via Duomo 147

San Gennaro/Januarius
Patron saint of blood banks
Saint's day:
19 September

The residents of Naples "seem to dwell on the confines of paradise and hell-fire."
—Edward Gibbon, 1764

Michael Kelly
1764–1826
An Irish tenor and composer, Kelly went to Naples at age 15 to learn opera singing.

2 This estimate comes from the Naples tourist office. Ida Pfeiffer, visiting in 1842, was told there were more than 300 churches.

St. Gennaro!"—"You pig of a Saint!"—"Barone maladetto!"—"You cursed rascal!"—"Cane faccia gialutta!" —"You yellow-faced dog!" In the midst of this, the blood (thanks to the heat of the Archbishop's hand) dissolved. They again threw themselves on their knees, and tearing their hair, (the old ladies particularly), with streaming eyes, cried, "Oh! most holy Saint, forgive us this once, and never more will we doubt your goodness!"

"Naples is a paradise; everyone lives in a state of intoxicated self-forgetfulness, myself included. I seem to be a completely different person whom I hardly recognize. Yesterday I thought to myself: Either you were mad before, or you are mad now."—Goethe, *Italian Journey,* 1787

The Duomo's ceiling paintings of Judith and the brazen serpent were done by Luca Giordano, apparently in 48 hours. This feat may have earned him his nickname Fra Presto.

Seekers of human interest will sit on the stairs outside and watch the activity on Via Duomo. Children play in the small piazza, dogs chase plastic bags, and girls strut their stuff, but most fascinating of all are the Duomo U-turns. Because of a short no-parking zone in front of the church, drivers along this crowded road feel confident in turning their cars around. Astoundingly, most motorists, cyclists, and pedestrians accommodate them.

For a souvenir of your visit to Naples's churches, look for the *presepi,* miniature Nativity scenes, found in abundance on nearby Via San Gregorio Armeno. In the 1780s, some of these cost up to £2,000, according to 18th-century traveler Hester Piozzi. A medium-size angel now goes for around $250, and a crèche with numerous figures for thousands. The figure shown here is for those on a tight budget.

Museo Archeologico
Nazionale
Piazza Museo
Nazionale 19

"I lighted by mistake
on a small room in
the museum of which
I still think with
horror . . . it requires
a strong mind like my
own to bear sights of
that kind. What is
Naples' censor about
that such figures are
not confiscated? Or
let separate days for
ladies and gentlemen
be arranged, so as to
give the matter at least
a scientific appear-
ance. Of one thing,
however, I am quite
convinced, the
Pompeiians were a
nice lot!"—
Wilhelmine Buchholz,
1887, after sneaking
into the "Reserved
Cabinet"

A MUSEUM OF MARVELS

The highlight of the Museum of
Archaeology is, without doubt, the
Farnese Collection, most notably *Hercules*
(background) and the "Farnese Bull,"
two Greek sculptures unearthed at or near
Rome's Baths of Caracalla in the mid-1500s,
then brought to Naples in 1786 after residing
at the Palazzo Farnese in Rome.

When first discovered, *Hercules* was legless.
The Farnese family asked Michelangelo to
make a set, but he refused, declaring himself
unworthy of the task. Guglielmo della Porta
obliged, but the original legs were found later
in a well on the Borghese estate and reunited
with their rightful body. The group known as
the "Farnese Bull" shows Zetheus and
Amphion, two brothers who tie Dirce, after
she mistreated their mother, to a raging bull.

The mosaics and Pompeiian frescoes are also
worth viewing, especially before going to
Herculaneum and Pompeii. The collection's
"Reserved Cabinet," also known as the *raccolta
pornografica,* pornography collection, has
recently reopened after being inaccessible for
decades. In the 19th century, male visitors only
were permitted to view its wonders but were
too gentlemanly to describe the place.

Excursion from Naples: Herculaneum

On the 24th of August, in A.D. 79, Vesuvius erupted with an astounding explosion after having teased the surrounding inhabitants for years with convulsions. On that day, the sea rose suddenly and flung fish onto the shore. Birds flying into the sulfurous vapor dropped from the sky; people and animals fell in fatal swoons. Tremors caused buildings to collapse. No lava flowed, but copious steam pouring out of the crater produced heavy rain. Mixed with volcanic dust, it caused a thick mudflow that buried towns. Subsequent eruptions produced lava and even more destruction, especially of Herculaneum.

Herculaneum, a resort of wealthy Romans close to Naples, was deeply buried. It was rediscovered—during the sinking of pits—in 1709, and excavations began in earnest 30 years later. Work continued through the century, but under King Ferdinand II, who ruled Naples intermittently from 1759 to 1825, prisoners of war chained together so tightly they could barely move were employed as diggers. During the course of these excavations, murals were removed, little cataloguing was done, and many objects were destroyed or stolen. Ferdinand's methods incurred the wrath of Rome's Director of Antiquities, Johann Winckelmann.

Herculaneum— Ercolano in Italian— is 12 km/7½ mi. from Naples. It is reached by the Circumvesuviana, a local train service that leaves from the annex of the Naples Centrale train station. Pompeii is farther on, along the same line, about 24 km/15 mi. from Naples.

BACKGROUND: *Artifacts from Herculaneum and Pompeii at the Museo Archeologico Nazionale.*

Teatro San Carlo

Piazza del Plebiscito, on the north side of the Palazzo Reale

"The *San Carlo* is a masterpiece of operatic architecture, provided that the curtain remains *down*!"—Stendhal, 1817

BACKGROUND: *The Neapolitan serenade,* O sole mio, *composed by E. di Capua in 1898, was adopted by Venetian gondoliers.*

FACING PAGE: *One of Naples's most enduring characters is Pulcinella or, as some visitors like to call him, Punchinella. He is thought to have been created in the 17th century by Puccio d'Aniello. This clown was a principal character in commedia dell'arte and a prototype of the English Punch.*

OPENING NIGHT AT SAN CARLO

San Carlo Theater, founded in 1737, was nearly consumed by fire in 1816 but was back in business less than a year later with a grand new design, featuring an auditorium garlanded in gold and silver. One eyewitness, Stendhal, was there opening night. The opera-hungry crowd, he reported, was so frantic that he lost the tails of his coat. Once everyone settled in, as well as Neapolitans can be said to "settle," the audience noticed smoke rising. Given the fate of their previous opera house, this was enough to launch a panic, but it soon became apparent that the new building had been overly damp and was steaming up with the heat of the crowd.

Stendhal was so excited that he forgot to mention which opera was performed until a few days later. It was *Il sogno di Partenope, Parthenope's Dream,* specially written for the opening by Johann Simone Mayr, a prolific composer and an influence on Rossini. The libretto was by journalist and playwright Urbano Lampredi. It was, Stendhal opined, "the grossest vein of sixteenth-century flattery; the text has not a redeeming feature, no more than has the music." The public has agreed with Stendhal; the opera is no longer performed.

By the 1840s Naples had some half-dozen theaters, but the San Carlo remains the most important.

The English naval hero Lord Nelson is remembered not only for his battles against Napoleon but also for his notorious affair with Lady Emma Hamilton, the beautiful and capricious wife of William Hamilton, a famed vulcanologist and British ambassador to Naples.

Nelson met Emma briefly in 1793 and became a close friend upon his return in 1798, when the French invaded Naples and joined with rebels fighting to establish a republic. Nelson helped King Ferdinand IV and other fugitives, including the Hamiltons, escape to Palermo. Nelson and Emma became lovers in 1800, and she bore his child a year later.

Nelson's triumph at Trafalgar has overshadowed his meddling in the revolt. When the French, defeated in northern Italy, left Naples, Nelson returned and carried out savage reprisals against the rebels. Under his orders, some hundred merciless executions took place in what historians describe as a "reign of terror."

A Famous Visitor
ALEXANDRE DUMAS, PÈRE: 1802–70

*W*hen Fench author Dumas was refused a visa to Naples in 1835, he borrowed someone else's passport. While in Naples, he became passionately involved with opera singer Caroline Unger, a Hungarian contralto who sang in Bellini's *Norma* and who had an understanding with a good friend of Dumas's. The affair started in Dumas's small boat during a violent squall (with the friend also on board) as the trio headed for Sicily. When Dumas returned to Naples, he was arrested and expelled for traveling with a false passport.

In 1860, Dumas became a gunrunner for Garibaldi. As a reward, he made himself director of Naples's museums and excavations. It was a short-lived career, lasting less than four years. He had greater success as the author of some 1,200 works, including *The Count of Monte Cristo* and *The Three Musketeers*.

Excursion from Naples: Virgil's Tomb
VIRGIL (PUBLICUS VERGILIUS MARO): 70–19 B.C.

$\mathscr{R}$oman poet Virgil died at Brundisium (Brindisi) but was buried at a site now just beyond Via Mergellina at the southwest extremity of the city. His tomb was a source of inspiration to Petrarch and to Boccaccio, who gave up commerce for poetry on the spot.

Tomba di Virgilio
Atop Galleria di Posillipo
Metro: Mergellina

Cimitero Protestante
The cemetery where Lady Craven lies has not been located. Two possibilities are:

Santa Maria della Fede
Piazza Santa Maria della Fede

Albergo dei Poveri
Piazza Carlo III

By 1840 whatever was left of the tomb was replaced by the Queen of France with what W. D. Howells called "an *exact* replica." A laurel tree had shaded the entrance but is said to have expired with Dante's last breath. Petrarch planted a replacement, which was stripped by relic hunters, including Lady Craven, who sent a branch to Frederick the Great. Yet another was planted by Casimir Delavigne, and another since, by someone else. The urn containing the poet's ashes was removed sometime in the 15th century, then lost. The tomb's former site may not be poetically inspiring, but the view is worth the excursion.

Lady Craven (notorious for adultery and wanderlust) was a longtime Naples resident. She complained that an Englishwoman not only had buried her dog near Virgil's tomb but also had erected a memorial stone to the animal. English herself, though married to a German aristocrat, Craven died in 1828 and was buried in Naples's Protestant Cemetery.

Studio Taormina   SICILIA

Sicilia

MAYBE YOU'RE THINKING OF going to Sicily for all kinds of noble reasons: to explore Greek ruins, to comprehend the Norman fascination with the Saracens, or to study Roman mosaics. But you may as well face it now. All of your good intentions will evaporate once you've sat down to your first meal, or even approached the first *pasticceria,* pastry shop. Food may not be the primary motivation to visit Sicily but, except for the most abstemious of travelers, it becomes the unquestioned highlight.

In Sicily more than anywhere else in Italy, food tells stories. Bits of bodies—saints' breasts or eyeballs, for example—are eaten on special days. Norma, the heroine of a Bellini opera, is recalled in Catania every time mouthfuls of a dish made of pasta, eggplant, and tomato are consumed.

Cassata, one of Sicily's ubiquitous sweets, was once made by nuns so possessed by perfecting it that the Church at one point forbade them from making more. Its ingredients are ricotta, pistachios, chocolate, candied fruit, and sponge cake. The sharp tang of the ricotta plays off the sweetness of the fruit and sugar. Another sweet is *cannoli,* rolled crêpes stuffed with a creamy ricotta and candied fruit mix. A good *cannolo* will ooze all over your face, hands, and shirt front.

"To have seen Italy without having seen Sicily is not to have seen Italy at all, for Sicily is the clue to everything."
—Goethe, *Italian Journey,* 1788

PREVIOUS PAGE: *A resident of Taormina poses for a studio shot with an unusual set of props, c. 1920.*
BACKGROUND: *Sicily, 1887.*

Carro Siciliano

Marzipan, though not exactly scrumptious, is a feast for the eyes. An incredibly sweet art form that imitates nature, it is made of colored sugar and almond paste molded into overgrown fruits and deceptively realistic fish, spaghetti, and flowers.

At the markets, if the quantity of food is startling, the colors are more so: you'll find huge trays of baked pearl-white onions, gray-green artichokes, and green and red peppers, as well as bushels of dark purple asparagus, the thick *asparagi neri*. Tomatoes, woven into garlands, are lushly and unexpectedly red, as though created from a crimson hue granted only to Sicily.

Food leads the visitor into the very essence of Sicily. Although important everywhere else in Italy, here it takes on an almost mythological status. For with the food, as in all its aspects, Sicily is Italy in a microcosm, intensified by the visible layers and amplified by sound and heat.

"This violence of landscape, this cruelty of climate, this continual tension in everything, and these monuments, even of the past, magnificent yet incomprehensible because not built by us and yet standing around like lovely mute ghosts; all those rulers who landed by main force from every direction, who were at once obeyed, soon detested, and always misunderstood, their only expressions works of art we couldn't understand and taxes which we understood only too well and which they spent elsewhere: all these things have formed our character."
—Giuseppe Tomasi di Lampedusa, *The Leopard,* 1958

Siracusa

*C*hronologically, it makes sense to start a tour of Sicily in the southeast, at the port city of Syracuse, where Corinthian Greeks, who had already established small colonies around Sicily, settled in 734 B.C. They lived mainly on the island of Ortygia (background)—now a fascinating warren of narrow streets and medieval and Baroque buildings. When they arrived, they encountered the original inhabitants, Sicanians, Elymmians, and Siculians, but they brought culture, science, building, and law to the island. Their colonies were frequently invaded by covetous Carthaginians and jealous Athenians and at last fell to the Romans in 210 B.C.

The first "Sicilian banquet" may have been the one given by Dionysius I, at which his guest, the courtier Damocles, was seated under a sword suspended by a single strand of hair. It was punishment for having exaggerated Dionysius's happiness.

GREEK SYRACUSE

One of Syracuse's many tyrants was Dionysius I, who ruled with absolute authority from 405 to 367 B.C. He repulsed Carthaginians, battled Siculians, formed alliances with Sparta and Athens, and made Greek Sicily a formidable power. He commanded loyalty from his slaves and mercenaries but feared retribution from enemies and contrived a fake assassination to justify hiring a bodyguard. Under him, military technology advanced with the building of better ships and siege machines, such as the catapult.

For all of his tyranny, Dionysius was a learned man who surrounded himself with poets and wrote his own poetry. He won a prize for his verse in Athens but died in the celebratory debauchery that followed. His son, Dionysius II, had few of his talents.

A Famous Syracusan
ARCHIMEDES: c. 287–212 B.C.

*A*cting nothing like the mathematician he was, Archimedes burst out of his bath one day and ran naked down the street yelling "Eureka!" (I found it!) While soaking, he'd been contemplating the water level of the bath and was suddenly struck with the understanding of specific weight. His other mathematical achievements included demonstrating the definition of the square root, solving cubic equations, and calculating the area and circumference of the circle. He was an engineer as well and discovered the center of gravity, the law of the lever, and the inclined plane. He also invented the "Archimedes Screw" (right) a device for transporting water upward, from a low level to a higher one.

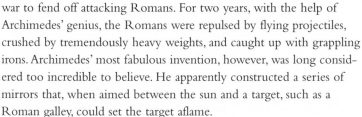

Archimedes was employed by Hiero, the king of Syracuse, who was a friend and possibly a relative, to devise machines of war to fend off attacking Romans. For two years, with the help of Archimedes' genius, the Romans were repulsed by flying projectiles, crushed by tremendously heavy weights, and caught up with grappling irons. Archimedes' most fabulous invention, however, was long considered too incredible to believe. He apparently constructed a series of mirrors that, when aimed between the sun and a target, such as a Roman galley, could set the target aflame.

When the Romans finally broke through Syracuse's well-defended walls, Archimedes was accidentally stabbed by a soldier, despite orders from General Marcellus to spare him.

Catacombe di San Giovanni
Evangelista
Via di San Giovanni

Santa Lucia
Syracuse's patron saint
Festa di Santa Lucia:
13 December and first
Sunday in May
Piazza del Duomo,
Ortygia

Santa Lucia al Sepolcro
Piazza Santa Lucia

ROMAN SYRACUSE

The most poignant remains of the Romans
are the catacombs used for Christian burials
at San Giovanni Evangelista. Laid out like an
underground city, this warren of lanes and
tombs is so extensive that a professor and his
six pupils, wandering through at the end of
the 19th century, became lost and died. Today,
a guide makes sure you don't stray.

Another reminder of Roman rule is Santa
Lucia, who, it is said, after pledging her life
to God, plucked out her eyes to give to an
admirer. According to another version of the
story, she was blinded by her persecutors. In
either case, she is often portrayed carrying her
eyes. After being denounced as a Christian in
A.D. 304, she survived many attempted punish-
ments—first court-ordered prostitution, then
burning at the stake. She eventually died from
a sword wound to the neck. Her body was
stolen and taken to Constantinople, then stolen
again and taken to the Church of Santa Lucia
in Venice. (Repeated pleas for the saint's
return to Syracuse have fallen on deaf ears.)
In Syracuse, her statue is carried in public
procession on 13 December and put on public
display at Santa Lucia al Sepolcro for eight
days. Celebratory food that day includes *cuccia,*
a pudding of grain and honey, as well as small
sweet buns shaped to resemble eyes.

Palermo

*T*here are few cities in the world with a setting as lovely as that of Palermo, with its abundance of forest, sky, and sea. Perched on the extreme northwest edge of the island, overlooking the Mediterranean, Palermo is in a valley called the Conca d'Oro, the Golden Shell. If the gods put their ears to the *conca,* they would hear the roar of the surf; mortals are treated to the bedlam arising from the city itself.

The delights of Palermo cut straight to the senses. The eye, for example, feasts on buildings influenced by North Africa; Baroque intrusions on these edifices turn the expected topsy-turvy.

The other senses, too, are cosseted by the city, but none more than taste. Sample a glass of *spremuta di limoni,* fresh lemon juice mixed with coarse sugar and served in a glass with its rim coated in salt. Be daring and try a *panino milza e ricotta,* made from veal sweetbreads and ricotta from the Antica Focacceria San Francesco. Or give in to what you've wanted to do all along and eat some gelati. If you go to Da Ciccio, you'll discover the finest ice cream in Italy and a superb sampling of all strata of Palermo society. Everyone comes here: businessmen, housewives, school kids, truckers, prostitutes, all consuming vast quantities of *gelati con panna,* ice cream with whipped cream, the most sinful dessert ever devised. But who cares about sin when you're in Palermo?

Antica Focacceria San Francesco
Via A. Paternostro

Da Ciccio
Corso dei Mille 73

BACKGROUND: *Palermo, 1892*

North Africa in Palermo Itinerary

Palermo's Moorish tradition lives on in buildings erected by the Normans. The following edifices were built in the 12th century by either the powerful and tolerant Roger II, his son William the Bad, or his grandson William the Good. Their austere exteriors barely hint at the splendor to be found within. Gilt mosaics; intricate *muqarna,* stucco sculptured into honeycombs (left); and Moorish arches are features of them all. Except Monreale, all are within walking distance of central Palermo.

PALAZZO REALE (PALAZZO DEI NORMANNI), CAPPELLA PALATINA: *Piazza Indipendenza*

The grandest of all Palermo's Norman buildings, the Royal Palace was constructed by Roger II in 1132. Within the Palatine Chapel, with its Moorish details, is an immense and glittering mosaic of Christ Pantocrator (Ruler of All), who looks down from the central apse. The chapel is the only part of the palace accessible without joining a guided tour, as the building is now used for the Sicilian parliament.

CASTELLO DELLA ZISA: *Piazza Guglielmo il Buono*

The citadel of Zisa (from al-Aziz, the Splendid, or Beloved) was begun by William the Bad and finished by William the Good. Restored after partially collapsing in 1971, it now showcases Arab art.

LA MARTORANA (CHIESA DI SANTA MARIA DELL'AMMIRAGLIO)
CHIESA DI SAN CATALDO: *Piazza Bellini 3*

First built in 1143 by the emir, or admiral, to Roger II, the Martorana displays a mix of Saracen, Norman, and Gothic styles, with some over-the-top Baroque. The adjacent San Cataldo, built 20 years later, is opened on demand. It has three red domes and Arabic inscriptions.

DUOMO DI MONREALE: *Piazza Duomo, Monreale*

This beautiful cathedral and cloister were built by William the Good in 1172. It is massive, much larger than the Cappella Palatina, and shares many of the same features, though it has been heavily restored. The adjacent cloister is encircled by columns, each one unique. The town of Monreale is 7 km/4½ mi. southeast of Palermo, a short bus trip from Piazza Indipendenza.

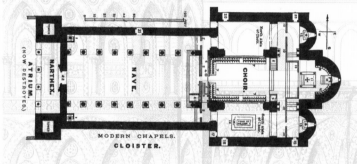

The Normans also produced the beautiful and much admired Rosalia, niece of William the Good, who was so dismayed at the prospect of marriage to Prince Baldwin that she became a hermit. She died in 1169 and, in 1624, her bones were found in her former dwelling—a cave on Monte Pelligrino—just in time for them to be used as talismans against the plague then raging through Palermo. Ever since, she's been celebrated as Palermo's savior and patron saint.

Santa Rosalia

Festino di Santa Rosalia: 10–15 July (dates shift slightly from year to year)

FACING PAGE: *From the ceiling in the Cappella Palatino, Palazzo Reale.* THIS PAGE: *Duomo di Monreale.*

Pier delle Vigne

Frederick II arrested
his friend and chief
counselor, scholar and
poet Pier delle Vigne,
on suspicion of
treachery. In despair,
Pier dashed out his
brains. His suicide got
him a place in Dante's
Inferno (Canto 13).
Pier has been credited
with creating the son-
net form.

BACKGROUND: *The
Crusades, Normans vs.
Saracens.* M. Meredith
Williams, 1910.

THE WONDER OF THE WORLD

Frederick II of Hohenstaufen was the last of the
Normans and one of Sicily's most enlightened
rulers. In 1196, two-year-old Frederick was
elected King of Rome. Two years later, he was
crowned King of Sicily (he became king officially in 1220). He added a third crown in 1212,
when he became king of the German throne in
Mainz. He led the Fifth Crusade, but not until
after several delays, for which he was excommunicated (one of three times). In the Holy
Land, he crowned himself King of Jerusalem.

Frederick was known as *Stupor mundi,* wonder
of the world, by almost everyone except supporters of the pope, with whom he frequently
clashed on matters of authority. As well, his
close ties with Muslims also raised the hackles
of the Church. Brilliant and ruthless, he took
daily baths, traveled with exotic pets, and kept
a Saracen harem. He founded the University
of Naples in 1224 and filled his court with
intellectuals. He wrote poetry and a book on
falconry, *De arte venandi cum avibus.* His legal
reforms ensured that common people were
judged by qualified judges and not their feudal
overlords. He died in 1250 from natural causes
and was immortalized by Dante, who put him
in the Inferno for heresy (Canto 10). It's said
that he will reappear at the end of time.

Catacombe dei Cappuccini

"A scene of inexpressible ghastliness."—*Murray's Guide to Southern Italy*, 1892

*T*hese catacombs were originally built in the late 16th century for Capuchin friars. The first to be embalmed and posed in his best habit was Fra' Silvestro da Buggio. Well-heeled Palermitans, however, coveted such a resting spot, and soon nonclerics were interred there, too. Individuals, couples, and entire families—some even holding what's left of their hands—are displayed in their finery. The last cadaver accepted was in 1881, with the exception of two-year-old Rosalia Lombardi, who was embalmed in 1920 with such realism that her appearance still astonishes with its vitality. The embalmer, Dr Solafia, died before he could reveal his incredible technique.

Alexandre Dumas, on a visit in 1860, noticed that the oldest cadaver was a Frenchman named Jean d'Esachard, who died at the age of 102. He also mentioned Francesco Tollari, who was propped up near the door, brandishing a club. Dumas was told that Tollari had been elevated to the position of concierge and that his club was to help him prevent any of the other cadavers from leaving.

Because even the dead wear out their clothes, families of the inhabitants of the catacombs used to descend on All Souls' Day (1 November) to deck out the embalmed in new attire. This practice ended around 1892, so the outfits worn by the hundreds of cadavers are steadily disintegrating, adding to the surreal horror of the place.

Convento dei Cappuccini
Via Cappuccini 1

A Famous Palermitan
ALESSANDRO, CONTE DI CAGLIOSTRO: 1743–95

$\mathcal{A}$ legend persisting since the 1790s identifies Giuseppe Balsamo, the celebrated hoaxer of Palermo, as Alessandro Calgiostro, a man who was said to have spent his childhood in the Arabian city of Medina. Balsamo was a quack, forger, and thief; Cagliostro, his alter ego, was a quack, alchemist, and Masonic spiritualist.

The Alley of Cagliostro
behind Hotel Cortese
Via Scarparelli 16

"The mention of Cagliostro always suggests the marvellous, the mysterious, the unknown. There is something cabalistic in the very sound of the name that, considering the occult phenomena performed by the strange personality who assumed it, is curiously appropriate. As an *incognito* it is, perhaps, the most suitable ever invented."
—W. R. H.
Trowbridge, *Cagliostro,*
1910

The story claims that, having been caught committing a variety of crimes, including forgery, the high-spirited Balsamo fled to Naples, assumed the name Cagliostro (among others), and married. Touting his young and equally roguish wife, Lorenza Feliciani, as being 60 years old, he sold elixirs of youth to the gullible Neapolitan high society. He passed himself off as more than 1,700 years old, crediting his elixir for giving him the chance to witness the crucifixion of Christ.

Some believe, however, that Cagliostro had nothing to do with Balsamo and that the real Cagliostro was wealthy beyond belief; lived in London, Paris, and Switzerland; and was worshiped for his telepathy and miracle cures. A hobnobber with royalty, Cagliostro fell from favor when he became a key player in a scandal that helped topple the French monarchy and led to his own downfall, fueling rumors that he was the notorious Balsamo. Jailed, then thrown out of France, he fled, ending up in Italy, where he was condemned to death for heresy. His sentence was commuted to life imprisonment in 1791. He lived out his remaining four years in the Fortress of San Leo in Urbino.

Goethe wrote the Cagliostro-inspired *Der Grosskophta* (1791) after visiting Balsamo's family in Palermo in 1787. They told him they were convinced that Balsamo and Cagliostro were one and the same man. Their house was situated in a lane, not far from today's Corso Vittorio Emanuele. Follow a small, hand-

painted sign posted on this street to a mangy alleyway near the Ballarò market that lays claim to Cagliostro. Hotel Cortese, backing on this wretched passage, calls itself the "house of Cagliostro."

Excursion from Palermo: Villa Palagonia

"*B*eggars of both sexes, men and women of Spain, Moors, Turks, hunchbacks, deformed persons of every kind, dwarfs, musicians, Pulcinellas, soldiers in antique uniforms, gods and goddesses, persons dressed in French fashions of long ago, soldiers with ammunition pouches and leggings."

Villa Palagonia
Piazza Garibaldi 3,
Bagheria

Johann Wolfgang von Goethe

1749–1832
The author of such dramas and poems as *Faust* and *Werther* toured Italy from 1786 to 1788. He visited Venice, Naples, and Sicily and lived for a time in Rome, associating with the artists and writers who congregated there. The strong Greek influence in Sicily affected him powerfully and inspired his *Nausicaa,* a never-finished version of the *Odyssey.*

So Goethe described the statuary in Villa Palagonia's garden. His words must have sent hundreds of tourists scurrying there and, amazingly, almost 220 years after his visit, this private home is still open to the public.

Built beginning in 1715 by Don Francesco Ferdinando Gravina e Crujlla, the fifth Prince of Palagonia, it wasn't finished until 1749. The villa is splendid enough, with its odd layout, grand staircase, and hall of mirrors, but the decorations that Goethe wrote about are what attract visitors. These were the work of the eccentric Francesco Ferdinando Gravina e Alliata, the seventh Palagonia Prince. Carved from soft volcanic tufa stone, they represent ladies and gentlemen, mythical and grotesque caricatures, and animals, mostly imaginary and monstrous.

Goethe was both annoyed and fascinated by the villa. He despised the immoral sentiment behind it, calling it the work of a maniac "with a passion for deformed and revolting shapes." The folly was much more pronounced in Goethe's time. Some chairs had legs sawn off

at unequal lengths; others had spikes poking out of the seats. China cups and saucers were glued together. From a crucifix, embedded flat into the ceiling, hung a chain bearing the body of a praying man. He was presumably a model. Goethe is not clear on this point.

Time and the elements have eroded the tufa statues, lessening their impact, but for those with a taste for the bizarre, a visit is rewarding all the same. Like many sites in Sicily, the Villa Palagonia is often in a state of *restauro,* which is not to say in a state of being a restaurant but, rather, under repair, so call ahead. The few guidebooks that mention the place take delight in their obscure descriptions of how to reach it from the Bagheria train station (8 km/5 mi. east of Palermo).[1]

1 Editor's note: The author insists that confusion is part of the Palagonian experience and so refuses to clarify the route.

Vocabolario Siciliano

Chiudere: to close; *giorno di chiusura:* closing day; *chiuso per restauro:* closed for renovation

Feste nazionali, feste religiose: national or religious festivals

Mattanza: capture and killing of tuna fish

Omertà: conspiracy of silence; submission

Passeggiata: evening promenade

Pesci in faccia: fish in the face; someone who is so rude he would slap your face with a fish

Tombola: game like bingo

Vergogna: honor or shame

CUCINA SICILIANA

Giuseppe Tomasi di Lampedusa's epic novel *Il gattopardo, The Leopard,* may have been read more for its history of Sicilian food than for its chronicle of Garibaldi's takeover of Palermo in the 1860s. Featured in the novel is a mouth-watering dish of *maccheroni,* macaroni, served to the book's hero, Prince Fabrizio, and his family. The diners quiver in awe when the "towering macaroni pie," with its scent of sugar and cinnamon, is brought out. As the knife cuts into the golden crust, fragrant aromas escape, redolent of chicken, truffles, and ham.

The author, captivated by this description, set out to re-create *Maccheroni alla Lampedusa.* It turned out to be expensive and weird, with strong, discordant flavors. Instructions are not included to avoid leading others into the same foolishness, but here is a list of ingredients:

Cooked macaroni or penne
Cooked, chopped chicken meat and liver
Sliced hard-boiled eggs
Ham
Chopped tomatoes
Grated or sliced black truffles
Caciocavallo or parmesan cheese
Demi-glace
Crust of flour, salt, sugar, and cinnamon

FACING PAGE: *Receipts from a real 19th-century* principe, *prince.*

Giuseppe Garibaldi
1807–82

Born in Nice, Italy's most remarkable patriot led revolts against the French, Piedmontese, and Austrians, but his greatest triumph was against the Bourbons in Sicily and Naples. Exiled frequently, he also fought in South America and made salami in New York.

Cacio: cheese; *come il cacio sui maccheroni:* to suit just fine

Il gattopardo was to have been released in January 1959, but, as the result of a favorable review that appeared early by mistake, the publishers had no choice but to send it out in late 1958. Fears that the book would be lost in the already saturated Christmas season were unfounded; it went on to become a best-seller, appealing to "delicate ladies of a certain age, 'angry young men,' and petit bourgeois who usually read the glossy magazines."

IL GATTOPARDO

Published in 1958, *The Leopard* was Giuseppe Tomasi di Lampedusa's only novel. Like his hero, Prince Fabrizio, Lampedusa was a Sicilian prince, only he traveled extensively, enlarging his world to the capitals of Europe. He finished the novel shortly before his death in 1957 and died not knowing if it would be published. It was considered a melancholy novel about a place and time that the world had forgotten and was called unpublishable. Luchino Visconti's 1963 film of the same name tackled the novel's complexities, creating a poignant testimony to the fading Sicilian aristocracy, in spite of an incongrous cast that included Burt Lancaster, Claudia Cardinale, and Alain Delon.

The Leopard's publisher, Giangiacomo Feltrinelli, also had the wisdom to publish *Doctor Zhivago,* after having the manuscript smuggled out of Russia. Both books became immensely successful. Feltrinelli, a zealous anti-capitalist, was from one of the richest families in Italy, and he used his fortune to launch numerous authors, through both his publishing company and his bookstores, which are now found in almost every Italian city. He was uncomfortable with his wealth and began assisting revolutionary groups. He died in 1972 when a bomb he had planted along an electrical line near Milan exploded prematurely.

Catania

The great volcano Mt Etna dominates the hectic east-coast port city of Catania. Situated just to the north and visible from most parts of the city, it has provided the hardened lava used in many of Catania's buildings. Because the city was largely destroyed in the 17th century, first by a massive eruption, then by an earthquake, most buildings date from that period, so Baroque rules.

The main street, Via Etnea, erupts every evening with the commencement of the *passeggiata,* promenade. The lively and loud conversations of the pedestrians battle with the roar of cars and buses. All here is noise and motion, intense and flamboyant, like a huge cocktail party held in the middle of a racing-car meet.

The town's patron saint is Sant'Agata, who suffered under Emperor Decius in A.D. 251, after rejecting the attentions of an unwanted, powerful suitor. She was beaten and burned, and her breasts were cut off (she stills carries them around on a plate). Then, just as she was about to die, an earthquake shook the land. The following year (and ever since) her veil was used to pacify Etna. Her body was taken to Constantinople in 1038 and returned in 1127. The Duomo was dedicated to her after the earthquake of 1693.

During her festival, bearers dressed in sackcloth carry her statue in procession, and everyone eats breast-shaped sweets, variously called *seni di vergine, minni di vergine,* or *cassatella.*

Festa di Sant'Agata
3–5 February

"Don Fabrizio asked for some ['virgins' cakes'] and, as he held them in his plate, looked like a profane caricature of St. Agata. . . . 'St. Agata's sliced-off breasts sold by convents, devoured at dances!'"—Giuseppe Tomasi di Lampedusa, *The Leopard,* 1958

BACKGROUND: *Catania, 1885.*

A Famous Catanian
VINCENZO BELLINI: 1801–35

Catania will not let anyone forget that
Bellini, the celebrated but short-lived
composer, was born here to a notable
family of composers. His birthplace
has been converted into the Bellini
Civic Museum, filled with mementos,
and a theater and gardens bear his
name. His operas include *Norma, Il
pirata, La sonnambula,* and *I puritani,*
written for Naples's Teatro San Carlo
and for Milan's La Scala. He was

Tomba di Bellini
Duomo
Piazza del Duomo

Teatro Massimo V. Bellini
Via Perrotta 12,
Piazza Bellini

Museo Civico Belliniano
Piazza San Francesco
d'Assisi 3

Giardino Bellini
Public gardens just off
Via Etnea

invited to
compose a
work for the
Paris Opera,
but after
moving to Paris in 1834, he fell ill and died the
next year, possibly of cholera. He was buried at
Père Lachaise in Paris but was brought home
40 years later and reburied in the Duomo.

Many of Catania's excellent restaurants serve
delicious pasta alla Norma, often spaghetti
tossed with tomatoes and eggplant, and sprin-
kled with salty ricotta cheese. It is reputedly
named after *Norma,* a two-act tragic opera that
premiered at La Scala in 1831, with Giuditta
Pasta in the title role!

FERROVIA CIRCUMETNEA

It's a wonder that any visitor manages to ride the Circumetnea, the train that partially circles Mt Etna. Catania hotel lobbies display out-of-date schedules; guidebook maps pinpoint its closed-down station on Corso delle Provincie. Those going there will find weeds growing amid traces of track. "How long has this been abandoned?" the hapless traveler wails. Asking around, she is told, "It's closed today." And sure enough, it is! And tomorrow, and the next day, too. Here's a tip: the station is on Via Caronda, high up Via Etnea and off most maps. It is best reached by taking the Metropolitana to the Borgo station. From there it's a short walk.

Once you find the station, which looks like it's been there for decades, it will be clear that that every schedule ever consulted is wrong,[2] giving plenty of time for a tour of the attached bar/*tabaccheria* and the parking lot out back.

The train makes several stops until Randazzo, where those not staying may expect to walk to the FS (Ferrovie della Stato) station to catch an onward train. But this station, too, has long been forsaken. Another futile walk and missed connection would have been avoided by hanging tight at the first station.

2 The charming fellow at the tourist information office denies the existence of a timetable and asserts that the trains leave at least once an hour. Don't believe him.

Circumetnea
Via Caronda 352/a

Etna's local name, "Mongibello," from *monte* and *djebel,* essentially means "mountain mountain."

BACKGROUND: *Mt Etna, 1878*.

Farewell

ALTHOUGH TRAVELS through Italy's idiosyncrasies could last forever, you have reached the end of this particular journey.

Thankfully, the guides remained faithful throughout, ensuring that your curiosity was ever piqued. You dallied with Byron, who saw the country as a stimulant; with Goethe, who relished enslavement to his sensations; and with Hester Piozzi, who cast a critical but loving eye over all she saw. You fretted with Wilhelmine Buchholz and learned much from Stendhal, who had actually declared that he traveled to Italy not for the serious purpose of studying the country, but for pleasure. Stendhal was being coy when he wrote that, as he realized that one of life's greatest pleasures is to come to know something and know it well.

And if what you've read in these pages, this mixture of legend, gossip, and *ben trovati,* has whetted your appetite for more, you can take pleasure in knowing that Italy herself awaits you, to eternally regale you with more of her improbable stories.

RIGHT: *A toast to the reader with a fiasco of Chianti.*

Image Sources

Uncredited images are from unidentified sources or private collections or have been credited in the caption.

Baedeker, Karl. *Central Italy.* Leipzig: Karl Baedeker, 1900: p. 113.
———. *Southern Italy.* Leipzig: Karl Baedeker, 1887: p. 172.
Ball, James Moores. *Andreas Vesalius: The Reformer of Anatomy.* St Louis: Medical Science Press, 1910: pp. 38, 79.
Barbiera, Raffaello. *La Principessa Belgiojoso.* Milan: Fratelli Treves, 1902: p. 34.
Boccaccio, Giovanni. *Contes de Boccace.* Paris: Barbier, 1846: p. 88.
Borromini, Francesco. *Opus architectonicum equitis Francisci Boromini.* Rome: S. Giannini, 1725: p. 142.
Browning, Oscar. *The Life of Bartolomeo Colleoni.* London: Arundel Society, 1891: pp. 23, 68, 69.
Burckhardt, Jacob. *Geschichte der Renaissance in Italien.* Stuttgart: Paul Neff, 1904: pp. 8, 9, 17 top, 36, 37, 62, 75 top, 84, 93 bottom, 103, 138 background.
Caffè Mokarabia logo, c. 1935: p. 30.
Casanova, Jacques (Giovanni). *The Memoirs of Jacques Casanova de Seingalt: Prince of Adventurers,* vol. 2. London: Navarre Society, 1922: p. 62.
Cellini, Benvenuto. *Memoirs of Benvenuto Cellini.* London: George Bell, 1893: p. 95.
Earle, Peggy: p. 7.
Eastlake, Charles L. *Handbook of Painting. The Italian Schools.* London: John Murray, 1869, vol. 1: pp. 116, 120; vol. 2: pp. 24, 80, 84–85.
Encyclopedia Britannica, Philadelphia: J. M. Stoddart, 1878, vol. 2: p. 173; vol. 8: p. 189; vol. 22: pp. 170–71.
Ente Nazionale Italiano per il Turismo (ENIT): pp. 35, 53.
Florimo, Francesco. *Bellini, Memoirie e Lettere.* Florence: G. Barbera, 1882: pp. 3 top center, 188.
Gibbon, Edward. *The History of the Decline and Fall of the Roman Empire,* vol. 1. London: John Murray, 1854: p. 144.
Griesbach, C. B. *Historic Ornament: A Pictorial Archive.* New York: Dover, 1975: pp. 17 bottom, 45, 51 bottom, 59 bottom, 93, 114–15, 176.

Hare, Augustus J. C., and St Clair Baddeley. *Venice.* London: George Allen, 1904: pp. 55 bottom, 56 bottom, 75 bottom.
Joyce Williams Prints and Maps: pp. 3 bottom right, 83.
Kapp, Julius. *Paganini.* Berlin: Schuster & Loeffler, 1921: p. 18.
Letarouilly, Paul. *Edifices de Rome moderne.* London: John Tiranti, 1928: pp. 129, 140.
Maurras, Charles. *Les amants de Venise: George Sand et A. de Musset.* Illustrations by Constant Le Breton. Paris: Les Maîtres du Livre, 1924: pp. iii, 54 bottom.
Meyer, Julius. *Antonio Allegri da Correggio.* London: Macmillan, 1876: p. 44.
Montagu, Lady Mary Wortley. *The Letters and Works of Lady Mary Wortley Montagu,* vol. 2. London: Richard Bentley, 1837: p. 81.
Murray's Handbook for Travellers in Southern Italy and Sicily, part 2. London: John Murray, 1892: pp. 175, 187.
Ojetti, Ugo. *I monumenti italiani e la guerra.* Milan: Alfieri & Lacroix, 1917, plate 4: p. 67.
Pater, Walter. *The Renaissance.* London: Macmillan, 1893: p. 136.
Pays, A.-J. du. *Italie et Sicile.* Paris: Librairie Hachette, 1874: backgrounds pp. 20–21, 54–55, 118–19, 124–25, 154–55.
Purcell, Rosamond: p. 39.
Rossetti, Maria Francesca. *A Shadow of Dante.* London: Rivingtons, 1871: p. 86 background.
Ruskin, John. *The Stones of Venice,* vol. 2. Sunnyside, Kent: George Allen, 1881: pp. 65, 71 top.
Sand, Maurice. *Masques et bouffons (Comédie italienne),* vol. 1. Paris: Michel Lévy, 1860: p. 165.
Symonds, J. A. *An Introduction to the Study of Dante.* Edinburgh: Adam & Charles Black, 1890: p. 52.
Trowbridge, W. R. H. *Cagliostro: The Splendour and Misery of a Master of Magic.* New York: E. P. Dutton, 1910: p. 181.
Young, G. F. *The Medici.* London: John Murray, 1913, vol. 1: p. 99 center; vol 2: p. 99 top right.
Vasari, Giorgio. *The Lives of the Painters, Sculptors & Architects.* London: J. M. Dent, 1900: pp. 97, 112 right, 116.

Notes

INTRODUCTION
1 Browning, line 175.
2 Byron quote in Moore, 239.
4 Campbell, xvi; Symonds 1888, 32.
5 Dante quote in Sayers, 82.

GENOVA
8 Heine, 92.
12 Buchholz, 51.
14 "pale, bloated" quote in MacCarthy, 347.
15 Moore, 172; Byron quote in Blessington, 106; Boswell quote in Brady et al., 18; Piozzi, 12, 55.

MILANO
20 Byron quote in Moore, 34; Gibbon, vol. 5, 352.
21 Gibbon, vol. 5, 352.
26 Dante quote in Sayers, 158, Canto 24, line 148.
27 Manzoni, 571.
28 Stendhal 1954, 411.
32 Barzini, 148.

BOLOGNA
36 Shelley quote in McMahan, 64; Byron quote in Moore, 150; Goethe, 115.
38 Cellini, 55.
43 Dickens, 108–9; Rogers, "Genevra."

FERRARA
48 Piozzi, 139.
49 Hugo, 229.
50 Shelley quote in Kuhns, 220.
51 Shelley quote in Moore, 352.
52 Browning, lines 611–12; "the characteristics," Rossetti, 31.

VENEZIA
54 Barbaro, 22; Byron quote in Moore, 44.

55 Shelley 1965 [1818], 335; Goethe, 77.
57 Venetian street words: Barbaro.
60 *Cook's,* 204.
62 Casanova, 3.
64 Piozzi, 127.
65 Ruskin, 164–65.
69 *Condotierri* details: Trease.
70 "finished a painting," Hauser, 238.
74 James, 72.
76 D'Annunzio, 218.

PADOVA
78 Baedeker 1928, 82; Howells, 212; Stendhal 1951 [1828], 39.
81 Curling, 228–30.
82 Petrarch quote in Hauser, 187.

FIRENZE
84 Dante quote in Hare 1907, 4; Howells 1884, 43; Dickens, 430; Symonds 1888, 119.
85 Dante quote in Hare 1907, 52; Twain, 253; McCarthy, 6.
86 "Behold," Kuhns, 41.
89 Vasari 1900 [1550], vol. 3, 254.
91 Eliot, 432–33.
92 Vasari 1991 [1550], 27.
93 Stendhal 1954, 442.
98 Ruskin quote in Hare 1907, 33–34.
104 Original jasmine chocolate details: Camporesi, 109–10.
106 Forsyth, 24; Starke, 67.

AREZZO
109 Lawrence, 21.
110 "Arezzo's accidental child," Forsyth, 56.
112 Vasari 1991 [1550], 163.

PERUGIA
115 James, 237; "bloody and licentious," Symonds 1904, 67.
116 Vasari 1991 [1550], 261.

PISA
118 Dickens, 154; Leopardi, 155.
119 Byron quote in Moore, 388.
120 Buchholz, 70; Dante quote in Rossetti, 97.
121 Stendhal 1959, 83; *condotierri* details: Trease; Machiavelli, 116.
122 Buchholz 66–67.

ROMA
124 Goethe, 149.
126 Buchholz, 70.
137 Starke, 155–56.
139 Buchholz, 95; Dickens, 394.
142 Forsyth, 99.
144 Gibbon, vol. 1, 84–85.
146 "It was the custom," Boswell quote in Brady et al., 16; Boswell's tour details: Brady et al.
147 Walpole quote in Hauser, 196.
148 Byron quote in Moore, 418.
150 Aretino quote in Chubb, 177.
152 "puckered face," Sayers, 254; "There was joy," Sayers, 259.

NAPOLI
154 Buchholz, 114; Piozzi, 218.
155 Leopardi, 195.
157 Hare 1883, 85.
160 Gibbon, vol. 1, 85; Kelly, 76.
161 Goethe, 207.
162 Buchholz, 113.
164 Stendhal 1959, 357.

SICILIA
170 Goethe, 246.
171 Tomasi di Lampedusa, 208.
179 *Murrays,* 309.
180 Trowbridge, 1.
182 Goethe, 239, 238.
185 Tomasi di Lampedusa, 76.
186 Feltrinelli, 177.
187 Tomasi di Lampedusa, 267.

Bibliography

Alighieri, Dante. *The Comedy of Dante Alighieri: Cantica II: Purgatory.* Translated by Dorothy L. Sayers. Harmondsworth: Penguin, 1949.

Annunzio, Gabriele D'. *The Flame.* Translated by Susan Bassnett. London: Quartet, 1991 (first published as *Il fuoco,* 1900).

Baedeker, Karl. *Central Italy.* Leipzig: Karl Baedeker, 1900.

———. *Italy: From the Alps to Naples.* Leipzig: Karl Baedeker, 1928.

Barbaro, Paolo. *Venice Revealed: An Intimate Portrait.* Translated by Tami Calliope. South Royalton, Vermont: Steerforth Italia, 1998 (first published as *La città ritrovata,* 1998).

Barzini, Luigi. *The Italians.* New York: Atheneum, 1964.

Bertarelli, L. V. *Northern Italy: From the Alps to Rome.* London: Macmillan, 1924 (first published in Italian by the Italian Touring Club).

Blessington, Marguerite, Countess of. *Conversations with Lord Byron.* Boston: William Veazie, 1859 (first published in *New Monthly Magazine,* 1832).

Boccaccio, Giovanni. *The Decameron.* Translated by Richard Aldington. Garden City, NY: Doubleday, 1932.

Brady, Frank, and Frederick A. Pottle, eds. *Boswell on the Grand Tour: Italy, Corsica, and France, 1765–1766.* London: William Heinemann, 1955.

Browning, Elizabeth Barrett. "Casa Guidi Windows," in *The Poetical Works of Elizabeth Barrett Browning.* London: Smith, Elder, 1897.

Buchholz, Wilhelmine. *The Buchholzes in Italy.* Edited by Julius Stinde, translated by Harriet F. Powell. London: George Bell, 1887.

Campbell, Thomas. *Life and Times of Petrarch,* vol. 1. London: Henry Colburn, 1843.

Casanova, Giovanni. *Casanova's Escape from the Leads.* Translated by Arthur Machen. London: Casanova Society, 1925.

Cellini, Benvenuto. *Memoirs of Benvenuto Cellini, A Florentine Artist; Written by Himself.* Translated by Thomas Roscoe. London: George Bell, 1893.

Cook's Traveller's Handbook, Northern Italy. London: Thomas Cook & Son, 1923.

Curling, Jonathan. *Edward Wortley Montagu, 1713–1776: The Man in the Iron Wig.* London: Andrew Melrose, 1954.

Dickens, Charles. *American Notes and Pictures from Italy.* Oxford: Oxford University Press, 1973 (first published 1846).

Eliot, George. *Romola.* London: Oxford University Press, 1971 (first published 1862–63).

Feltrinelli, Carlo. *Senior Service.* Translated by Alistair McEwen. London: Granta, 2001.

Forsyth, Joseph. *Remarks on Antiquities, Arts, and Letters during an Excursion in Italy, in the Years 1802 and 1803.* Edited by Keith Crook. Newark: University of Delaware Press, 2001.

Gibbon, Edward. *The History of the Decline and Fall of the Roman Empire,* vols. 1 and 5. Edited by William Smith. London: John Murray, 1854.

Goethe, Johann Wolfgang von. *Italian Journey [1786–1788].* Translated by W. H. Auden and Elizabeth Mayer. Harmondsworth: Penguin, 1962.

Hare, Augustus J. C. *Cities of Southern Italy and Sicily.* London: Smith, Elder, 1883.

———. *Florence.* Revised by St Clair Baddeley. London: George Allen, 1907.

Hare, Augustus J. C., and St Clair Baddeley. *Venice.* London: George Allen, 1904.

Hauser, Ernest O. *Italy: A Cultural Guide.* New York: Atheneum, 1981.

Hawthorne, Nathaniel. *The Marble Faun.* New York: Pocket Library, 1958 (first published 1860).

Heine, Heinrich. *Italian Travel Sketches.* Translated by Elizabeth A. Sharp. London: Walter Scott, c. 1892 (first published as *Reisebilder,* 1827–31).

Howells, W. D. *Italian Journeys.* Boston: Houghton Mifflin, 1895.

———. *Tuscan Cities.* Boston: Houghton Mifflin, 1884.

Hugo, Victor. *Lucrèce Borgia.* Paris: Nelson, 1930.

Italie. Paris: Guide Pratiques Conty, c. 1930.

James, Henry. *Italian Hours.* London: William Heinemann, 1909.

Kelly, Michael. *Reminiscences,* vol 1. New York: Da Capo Press, 1968 (first published 1826).

Kuhns, Oscar. *The Great Poets of Italy.* Boston: Houghton Mifflin, 1903.

Landor, Walter Savage. "On Seeing a Hair of Lucretia Borgia," in *New Monthly Magazine and Literary Journal,* July 1825.

Lawrence, D. H. *Etruscan Places.* New York: Viking, 1970 (first published 1932).

Leopardi, Giacomo. *A Leopardi Reader.* Edited and translated by Ottavaio M. Casale. Chicago: University of Illinois Press, 1981.

MacCarthy, Fiona. *Byron: Life and Legend.* London: John Murray, 2002.

McCarthy, Mary. *The Stones of Florence.* New York: Harcourt, Brace, 1959.

Machiavelli, Niccolò. *The Prince.* Translated by Peter Bondanella and Mark Musa. Harmondsworth: Penguin, 1979 (first published as *Il principe,* 1532).

McMahan, Anna B., ed. *With Shelley in Italy: A Selection of His Italian Poems and Letters.* London: T. Fisher Unwin, 1907.

Montagu, Lady Mary Wortley. *The Letters and Works of Lady Mary Wortley Montagu,* vol. 2. Edited by Lord Wharncliffe. London: Richard Bentley, 1837.

Moore, Thomas. *Letters and Journals of Lord Byron with Notices of His Life,* vol. 2. New York: J & J Harper, 1831.

Murray's Handbook for Travellers in Southern Italy and Sicily, Part II: Sicily. London: John Murray, 1892.

Piozzi, Hester (Lynch) Thrale. *Glimpses of Italian Society in the Eighteenth Century from the Journey of Mrs. Piozzi.* London: Seeley, 1892.

Rossetti, Maria Francesca. *A Shadow of Dante.* London: Rivingtons, 1871.

Ruskin, John. *The Stones of Venice,* vol. 2. Sunnyside, Kent: George Allen, 1881.

Shelley, Percy Bysshe. *The Complete Works,* vol. 9. Edited by Roger Ingpen. New York: Gordian Press, 1965.

Starke, Mariana. *Travels in Europe, For the Use of Travellers on the Continent.* Paris: Galignani, 1839.

Stendhal [Marie-Henri Beyle]. *Un Inédit de Stendhal, Guide à l'usage d'un voyageur en Italie.* Paris: Robert d'Illiers, 1951 [1828].

———. *The Private Diaries of Stendhal.* Translated and edited by Robert Sage. Garden City: Doubleday, 1954.

———. *A Roman Journal.* Translated by Haakon Chevalier. New York: Orion Press, 1957 (first published as *Promenades dans Rome,* 1829).

———. *Rome, Naples, and Florence.* Translated by Richard N. Coe. London: John Calder, 1959 (first published in French, 1818).

Symonds, J. A. *Renaissance in Italy: The Age of the Despots.* New York: Henry Holt, 1888.

Symonds, Margaret, and Lina Duff Gordon. *The Story of Perugia.* London: J. N. Dent, 1904.

Tomasi di Lampedusa, Giuseppe. *The Leopard.* Translated by Archibald Colquhoun. New York: Pantheon, 1960 (first published as *Il gattopardo,* 1958).

Trowbridge, W. R. H. *Cagliostro: The Splendour and Misery of a Master of Magic.* New York: E. P. Dutton, 1910.

Twain, Mark. *The Innocents Abroad,* vol. 1. New York: Harper & Row, 1911 (first published 1869).

Vasari, Giorgio. *The Lives of Artists.* Translated by Julia Conaway Bondanella and Peter Bondanella. Oxford: Oxford University Press, 1991.

———. *The Lives of the Painters, Sculptors & Architects.* Translated by A. B. Hinds. London: J. M. Dent, 1900 (first published as *Vite de' più eccellenti architetti, pittori et scultori italiani,* 1550).